The Power of Leadership
"Finding the Leader Within"

Unlocking the Door to True Success and
Happiness in Your Life.

By Daniel Sweet & Debbra Sweet

The Power of Leadership is a 12 Part Series.
If you would like to contribute a chapter to one or more of
the books in this series, then contact Daniel Sweet at Pro
Publishing Company for more information.

www.Pro-Publishing-Company.com
Email: support@pro-publishing-company.com

The Power of Leadership: Volume 1
"Finding the Leader Within"
By Daniel Sweet & Debbra Sweet

Published by Pro Publishing Company
Editing by Daniel & Debbra Sweet
www.Pro-Publishing-Company.com
Email: support@pro-publishing-company.com

ISBN 978-0-9818044-0-8
Printed in the United States of America, July 2008

Cover Design by Daniel & Debbra Sweet
Graphic Arts by James W. Guerrero, Daniel Sweet and Debbra Sweet
www.SweetMarketingSolutions.com

This book is designed to provide general information and entertainment to its readers on the subject of leadership. While all the stories and anecdotes described herein are based on true experiences, some of the names may be pseudonyms, some stories are compilations, and some situations may have been changed or edited for content, educational purposes and/or to protect each individual's privacy.

This book is sold, purchased and read with the understanding that neither the Publisher nor the Authors are engaging in the rendering of legal, business, personal or other professional services by publishing the information contained in this book. The use of these views and opinions is in no way intended to be a substitute for business, personal, legal, accounting, investment, medical and for any other professional advice or services you may require to suit your specific needs. Always consult a licensed professional for answers to your specific questions and unique situation. The Publisher and its contributing authors specifically disclaim any liability, loss, or risk that is incurred as a consequence, directly or indirectly of the use and application of any of the contents of this work.

The content of each chapter is the sole expression and opinion of its author, and is not necessarily that of the Publisher. No warranties or guarantees are expressed or implied by the Publisher's choice to include any of the content in this work. The information supplied to us by our contributors is believed to be reliable; however, such reliability cannot be guaranteed. We offer no guarantees as to the accuracy, timeliness or completeness of the information contained herein and disclaim any and all liability relating thereto. Pro Publishing Company is not responsible for any claims made by the contributing authors of this book.

Pro Publishing Company and the contributing authors contained herein shall not be liable for any contentions, damages or costs arising out of or in any way connected with the reader's use of the materials and information provided or accessed through this publication.

Table of Contents

Table of Contents

Chapter   **Page**

Section 5: Extra Insights to Great Leadership

"If your actions inspire others to dream more, learn more, do more and become more, you are a leader"

JOHN QUINCY ADAMS

Ivan R. Misner, Ph.D.

Called the father of modern networking by CNN, Dr. Ivan Misner is a New York Times bestselling author. He is the Founder and Chairman of BNI (www.BNI.com), the world's largest business networking organization.

His latest books, Masters of Sales and The 29% Solution can be viewed at www.MastersBooks.com and www.29percentsolution.com. Dr. Misner is also the Senior Partner for the Referral Institute, an international referral training company (www.referralinstitute.com). He can be reached at misner@bni.com.

Foreword

In the Introduction to this book, Daniel and Debbra Sweet state, *"True leadership reflects the ultimate ability to give. You give a part of yourself each time you serve and the best leaders know that their return is often the personal fulfillment in knowing that through leadership and giving, the leaders receive back in abundance"*. This statement refers to the universal law of reciprocity, summed up by the old adage "give and you shall receive," and for over twenty years I have been leading a very successful international organization based on practicing that law.

Having studied briefly under one of the world's leading experts on the topic at USC, Warren Bennis, I am absolutely convinced that the real power of leadership is in the ripple of positive effects which result when an individual influences others through serving as an example and guiding by empowering those they are leading.

The Power of Leadership is filled with insight from leaders who exemplify what it truly means to be a leader. They are beacons of strength and character who have dedicated themselves to succeeding by helping others to succeed. Their words, stemming from depths of experience, will teach you what it takes to build unwavering character and become a leader capable of achieving success for yourself and others.

We now live in a fully global society and there is no shortage of opportunities to help other people. People across the globe are more connected than ever and if you want to make a positive contribution to the lives of those you cross paths with and find more fulfillment in your own life, spend some quality time with this book and find your inner leader. Leadership opportunities abound everywhere and now is the time to take action.

Ivan R. Misner, Ph.D.
Founder of BNI
New York Times Bestselling Author

Introduction

Daniel & Debbra Sweet

This book is Volume 1 of a 12 Part Series on the Power of Leadership. We are dedicating this book to all seekers of greatness, the unique individuals who want to rise up from where they are in life right now and seek a brighter future. This can only be accomplished by first finding and developing the leader within themselves.

In this volume on Finding the Leader Within, you'll uncover personal stories of inspiration and instruction from other people, some maybe even just like you, who have gone from rags to riches – mentally as well as monetarily – and how you can too.

Leadership usually comes to most people because they are either thrust into it or they are willing to step forward and take on a leadership role. When one thinks of leadership, there is usually an understanding that along with the position in title and duty, responsibility and accountability to others comes along with it.

Being a leader is not always about being in business. People find challenges in their daily lives in many different ways. Leadership skills come in handy whether you are raising children, counseling a friend, looking for a job or dealing with an uncomfortable situation.

There are some who we have met who, unknowingly, walked with the propensity of dynamic leadership. They have inspired, taught, mentored and helped others to reach greatness without giving it much thought. Through the real life stories and heartfelt sharing in **The Power of Leadership:** *"Finding the Leader Within"* our goal is to inspire you to see that you too, have great leadership skills.

Some people are born with behaviors that emanate strong leadership tendencies. Others have learned how to be a leader.

There are people we have seen over the years who have displayed a heart to serve, to lead, to learn and to grow. Some of these people are stepping forward and taking on the mantle of leadership. Others will sit quietly on the sidelines hoping for the opportunity to give. They hope that someone will notice and offer them the chance to speak up. These quiet supporters of leadership are uncertain of how to make their heart to serve known.

This book is geared to inspire, encourage and support all of the above. Our goal is to share and teach, to guide and to give so that you too can confidently step forward becoming a strong leader in your own circle of influence.

The best leaders are not those who become leaders for the sake of power. The best leaders are those who serve others with their ability to make choices and decisions and then stand behind them. They walk with integrity in order to better the lives of the people they lead.

True leadership reflects the ultimate ability to give. You give a part of yourself each time you serve and the best leaders know that their return is often the personal fulfillment in knowing that through leadership and giving, the leaders receive back in abundance.

To become a leader of others you must first have learned to lead yourself. That takes discipline, dedication and a willingness to always go the extra mile. We all have an inner burning desire to better ourselves in some way. It takes commitment and tenacity.

Think about it. You personally have probably seen normal people do extraordinary things. Like the kid who finally stands up to the bully or the average guy who gets up the nerve to quit his job, follow his dreams and go into business for himself.

You've also seen extraordinary people do what seems like near supernatural feats. Like Martha Stewart going from downtrodden teenager to household name with national superstar status in only a few short years, end up in jail then rise from the ashes and make a major come back. Even Donald Trump went from middle class to ultra rich, to completely broke and back to very rich again – and even more famous than he was before!

As a young man, Abraham Lincoln was a dismal failure in business. He gave up his law practice and was forced into bankruptcy. As you well know, Mr. Lincoln later went on to become President of the United States and one of the most beloved one's at that!

Do you wonder how they did it? They found the leader within themselves and the courage to act on it. Not just thinking about it, but also taking action! That is the most crucial point in accomplishing goals.

You must take action… now. Not tomorrow, next week or later when you feel the timing is right. Do it now. Just like you are taking action by reading this book. You are one step closer to greatness just because you are taking action.

Leaders take immediate action. You can do this too. Smart leaders seek the guidance of others who have gone before them; so enjoy the true life examples in this book. The authors have given their story to you to share, guide and inspire. If you wish to contact any of the authors, please do so. They have graciously made themselves available to you by including their contact information.

Follow in their footsteps, learn from their mistakes, rejoice in your triumphs and you too can achieve greater things in life for yourself and for your loved ones.

Section 1:

Creating Your Foundation for Leadership

Daniel Sweet

Daniel Sweet is the creator and CEO of Pro Publishing Company and of the Power of Leadership book series. Daniel owes much of his knowledge and success in leadership to studying the Bible and to his mentor, a powerful man of God who is the founder of the Association of Christian Fellowships, Mr. R. Frank Tulak.

A dynamic and growth minded individual, Daniel Sweet has been an entrepreneur since 1978 at the early age of twelve years old. Since then he has been a professional musician and an award winning recording artist appearing on stage, radio and on TV. He has started and run a multi truck carpet cleaning company and published a monthly magazine among various other endeavours. He is currently the owner and CEO of Pro Publishing Company while simultaneously co-owning and operating an integrated communications marketing firm with his wife of 17 years, Debbra Sweet.

Daniel is also an active investor in real estate, owns several small online businesses and is an ordained minister. He is serving as President and Senior Pastor of a national Christian biblical research ministry found at www.GodsWordFirst.org.

Contact Info: support@pro-publishing-company.com
www.Pro-Publishing-Company.com

Chapter One

How Do We Define Leadership?

Daniel Sweet

Wherever you see a successful business, know that there is a leader making courageous decisions. This person walks the path that others dream of but fear to tread. The path to becoming a leader is actually a path of personal growth, learning how to utilize all of one's resources and becoming all that one can be.

Most believe that leadership is an innate quality that some have, not others. They believe that leaders are born not made. Nothing can be further from the truth. Each one of us has the potential to stand tall, be a light to others, clearly define a vision and mission and take charge. Within every individual, an "Inner Leader" is waiting to be born. So how are leaders different from the ordinary?

First, let us define leadership so that we are all on the same page. Leadership is the process by which a person influences others to accomplish an objective. Leaders have vision, which they share with others. The leader binds a group of people with beliefs, values and knowledge.

Many individuals think of a leader as having power over others. These leaders mistakenly use their power to dominate and control. This is not leadership, but domination. It is a sign of weakness, not strength.

True strength comes from understanding that the real function of a leader is to serve, to actualize a larger vision, and be dedicated to a cause beyond one's personal concerns. Rather than think that others are there to serve you, realize that each person on your team is someone you are there to help. It is your job to bring out the best in him/her. When you help them become all they can be, when you share your vision and bring it alive in them, you are truly leading.

This key can be implemented by putting your attention on the well-being of others, not just necessarily on your goal. Others, sensing your concern, feel cared for and uplifted. They naturally work to the best of their capacities and offer support in return.

True leadership is more of a relationship between the leader and the followers than it is about the person who is in charge. Leadership is lifting a person's vision to higher sights, the raising of a person's performance to a higher standard, the building of a personality beyond its normal limitations.

The foundation of this relationship is trust. Ethics refer to the principles that define behavior as right, good and proper. There is a strong link between leadership and ethics. Leaders must themselves be ethical in their decisions and actions in order to influence others to behave accordingly. On the other side, a leader with poor ethics will develop a following of people who produce strife, contention and little to no positive results.

Leadership is an art that you can master. It calls for you to raise your performance to higher standards and think outside your limitations. The basis of good leadership is character and the willingness to make sacrifices for the sake of the people in your organization. In short, it takes nerve!

Leaders, by definition, set examples for others to follow. However, before that happens, they will have to prove their worth. Those expected to follow are constantly observing leaders. For this reason, integrity and courage define leadership better than any pompous statement of job title, credentials or college degree!

Are You a Driver or a Leader?

The following is a true story about a leadership training seminar held by Joe Batten. He is an accomplished public speaker and member of the National Speaker's Association Hall of Fame. He wrote the best selling book titled: "Tough-Minded Leadership".

A number of years ago, Joe met with a group of 35 CEOs for a daylong seminar on his favorite subject, Leadership. Early in the presentation, he asked them, "How many of you are leaders in your company?" Every person in the room raised his hand. Joe smiled and said, "I'll ask you the same question after I share this true story with you."

In the Middle-East there are two countries, separated only by a border, who have large sheep and mutton industries. The cultures of the two countries are radically different and they are hostile to each other. In fact, they have even fought wars with each other.

In one country, the shepherds walk behind their flocks. In the other country, the shepherds walk in front of their flocks. Now remember, this is a true story.

In the country where the shepherds walk behind their flocks, the quality of the mutton and the wool is poor and it is not a profitable industry.

In the country where the shepherds walk in front of their flocks, the quality of the mutton and wool is excellent and the profitability is high.

Why?

In the flocks where the shepherd walks behind and pushes, drives, corrects, and is always in charge, the young sheep grow up afraid to stray from the flock for fear of being rapped up-side the head by the shepherd's staff or having the dogs sent out to round them up.

They have no opportunity to explore for better grass and water, or to play with other young lambs. They simply become obedient, passive and apathetic. By the time they are grown, they have lost all initiative. They are not really healthy.

In the country where the shepherds walk in front of their flocks, the young lambs have plenty of opportunity to stray, play, experiment, and then catch up to the flock. Instead of feeling overly controlled, compressed, repressed, depressed and suppressed, they feel free, empowered, enhanced and stretched. They eat more, sleep better and grow up large and healthy. They are truly led."

When Joe finished his story, assuring the executives once more of its authenticity, he asked again, "How many of you truly lead in your company?" Not a hand was raised.

The reason I told you Joe's story was to make a distinction between *Driving* an organization forward and *Leading* it toward success, and to let you know that that is a fundamental choice you can make. I feel it is the most important decision you have to make in order to succeed.

I say you are Driven by your fears and you are Led by your values and your vision. Leaders lead by virtue of their vision (and your vision is the experience and expression of your values). That is what people really follow- Vision. Nobody likes to be driven. As the leader in your organization, it is your duty to create, communicate and hold a powerful and empowering vision for yourself and your people.

Remember the moral of Joe's story. Driving your organization is not healthy; choose instead to lead by example guided by your vision.

Let us now analyze the ten major characteristic of a good leader.

1) Honesty - Reliable behavior on your part will win trust and respect from others.

2) Vision - You need to be able to see ahead and set goals for the future.

3) Inspiration - The best way to motivate others to reach new heights is to teach them to believe in themselves.

4) Intelligence - Learn from every situation, and from those who have a certain expertise that you might lack. Observe, ask questions and always be seeking knowledge - that is what true intelligence is all about.

5) Fair-mindedness - As a leader, it is much more important to be fair than to be popular. Playing favorites is a sure fire way to failing as a leader.

6) Open-mindedness - An open-minded leader is an effective one.

7) Boldness - You must have the nerve to take calculated risks and maintain the ability to stay calm and confident under pressure.

8) Imagination - Be creative in the way you set new goals, plans and methods.

9) Perseverance - In the words of Thomas Edison, "Our greatest weakness lies in giving up. The most certain way to succeed is always to try just one more time."

10) Courage of Conviction - It takes courage to deviate from the trodden path and lead people to success.

Now take a moment to find out what makes leaders thrive.

Leaders are risk-takers. They thrive on adversity and challenges but the more important attribute is that most of them are also capable of managing and mitigating their risk.

True leaders understand and appreciate that great things are rarely achieved single-handed - a team is required to achieve success. One of the traits of a truly great leader is their ability to build a powerful and successful team of like-minded people. Leaders succeed by helping people they work with become successful themselves.

Leaders are good listeners. It is a commonly held belief that leaders are impatient and rarely listen to others. In fact, the truth is the quite the opposite. They have the innate ability to foster good relationships among team members and have exceptional communication skills that inspire total commitment and follow through from their co-workers.

Leaders are quick decision makers. Strong leaders are quick on their feet when taking decisive action, great at making spontaneous decisions and good at long-term strategic thinking. It is their general awareness, alertness, the ability to read and analyze a situation and the tendency to think strategically that makes them the great leaders that they are.

Good leaders are not control freaks. It is true that one of the basic characteristics of leaders is their need to control things. However, what makes them different is the way they respond to stress. Their performance under pressure is what sets them apart from the crowd. Good leaders become effective leaders by being able to delegate responsibilities and inspire trust among the followers.

Conclusion

If you are seeking to become a stronger leader, you will have to show confidence, energy, determination, self-discipline, willpower, and spirit. Only then will you be able to motivate others and lead them to greater achievement. I believe everyone can improve their leadership skills, provided they follow a leader of their own.

Finding and developing the leader within yourself is more about the journey, not the destination.

Luckily, for you, expert guidance is available in the form of this book and by all the contributing authors herein. They are here for you; they have given you their contact information and are waiting for you to get in touch with them.

Allow them to guide you by reading their words and through personal interaction with them. Turn to them for guidance and you will be well on your journey to finding and growing the leader within yourself for greater health, wealth and prosperity.

Robert Vance

Robert Vance is a Husband, Father, and Coach. He has experienced success in several careers in his life. He currently runs a successful consulting company where he helps people achieve their dreams and desires. During his journey, he has learned a lot and has held on to his dreams. His passion to achieve those dreams drives him through life. It is his purpose in life to help other people achieve their goals and succeed in life.

He has experienced both the highs and lows that come with every success story. He has succeeded and failed several times in life. He believes you are not a failure until you give up on yourself.

Robert was born in Northern California and grew up in the Bay Area. He is currently living in the Los Angeles area and happily married to his lovely wife Lilly. They have 6 children ranging in age from 1 year to 21 years old. He enjoys spending time with his family, taking trips to the mountains, traveling around the US and discovering new places.

Email: robertvance@abundanceforlifetoday.com
Web: www.abundanceforlifetoday.com

Chapter Two

The Road to Leadership

Robert Vance

The road to leadership must begin with you. You must be willing to work on yourself in order to become a leader. Now do not get me wrong you can be a leader right now but if you want to increase your leadership you must be willing to get the training and educate yourself so that you move to the next level. As you improve yourself you increase your capacity to lead a more diverse group.

What kind of training am I talking about; well it is not the college education. While that is important it is not what makes a leader. What makes a leader is the personal development you do for yourself. The reading of books on how to improve, the taking of personal development courses; things to help you change the way you think.

My road to leadership began several years ago. It started by my desire to read books to improve my skills. Skills like communicating with people, changing your thoughts, and changing who you are. Some of these books include "How to Win Friends and Influence People", "Think and Grow Rich" and "Rich Dad Poor Dad". I also took some leadership development courses. In these courses I learned skills like how to trust people, Win-Win, Responsibility, Compassion, Service, Abundance, Honesty and Getting out of your comfort zone.

Lets talk about trust for a minute. Trust can be broken down into two things: do you trust others and do they trust you. If you do not trust others then it is very difficult for them to trust you. Trust is the foundation of relationships. If the people you lead do not trust you then they are going to be less likely to freely do what is asked. They may do it out of fear of the consequences but not because of you as the leader.

Here are some things for you to think about on trust. Do you trust other people and if so how far? Will you trust others with your life, money, or a deep secret? Will other people trust you with their money, life or a deep secret? Have you become so jaded that you do not trust anyone anymore? Are you trustworthy?

Win-Win is a concept that revolves around the belief that both parties can come out a winner. The people that operate from win-lose do so because they believe it must be either – or. It is possible that you both can get what you want and both win. When you operate from the belief that it has to be either-or you focus on one of you winning and the other losing. It is possible for both parties to win and everybody leaving the transaction feeling good about it. Even in a bad situation it is possible to have a Win – Win result.

Here is an example: someone is in a bad way with their house and has fallen behind in their payments. Someone wanting to help save their home contacts them. The person wanting to help will win because they get a home at a lower price than retail. The person behind in payments wins by saving their credit, getting some money for the equity they have in the home and a peace of mind from not having the mortgage holder call them.

Here are some things for you to think about on Win-Win. Do you operate from a position of win-win? What is the potential for growth if you change your thinking from win-lose, either-or to Win - Win? How different would the world be if everyone in it (The leaders, Those in position of Authority, You and I, Etc.) operated from win-win?

Responsibility is not the concept of being at fault. It is the position of being responsible for your actions regardless of the consequences. A person that is responsible believes that they make things happen by the choices they make. They do not believe things happen to them. A perfect example of responsible is a person who is pulled over for speeding. They have a choice. They can be responsible and say to themselves I made the choice to speed and these are the consequences of that choice. They could also choose to not take responsibility and say why did this happen to me.

Here are some things for you to think about on responsibility. Do you take responsibility for your choices or are you a victim to the things that happen to you? How would it change your life if you started to take responsibility?

Compassion is about wanting to help others. It does not mean you are weak or soft. Having compassion means you genuinely care about the people you lead and want to help them succeed in their ventures. If you help people get what they want you will get what you want. By having compassion for your constituents you show how much of a true leader you are.

Here are some things for you to think about on compassion. Who would it impact in your organization if you had true compassion for the people you lead? How could you impact your life, community, country or the world by having compassion?

Service is not something we do. It is a lifestyle we live. I would like to start off with a quote by William Churchill: *"We make a living by what we get. We make a life by what we give."* Most people live an ordinary life. There are some that live an astonishing life. These are the people that in addition to being highly successful in life make a great contribution to society, the people they come in contact with, and leave a legacy for future generations.

Being of service is not necessarily about giving money to those in need. It's about giving of your time, talent, or finances unconditionally without expectation of return or reward. The person living the astonishing life is always looking for ways to make their surroundings and the world a better place.

While there are some people that value their life above all else there are also those that value life above their own. Giving not only includes giving to others but also giving to yourself. If you do not take care of yourself you may come to the point where you feel like you cannot give any more and you get burnt out. Remember to take care of yourself so that you can continue to be of service to others.

Some people think that they must look out for them selves or no one else will. They live in a world where there are winners and losers. There are those that choose a different path and instead of seeing winners and losers they see a world whereby helping others win, they win as well. If you truly want to grow in life give what you have little of. By doing this you will increase your capacity in this area.

Here are some things for you to think about on Service. How can you impact your community, or the world with your service? How would the world change if everyone tried to be of service to others?

Abundance is a belief that there are unlimited resources you simply need to tap into so that you can help yourself and others. Most people believe there is not enough (time, money etc.) to go around. This comes from a scarcity line of thinking. By living in scarcity you truly limit yourself. You limit yourself by your fear of loss. You prevent yourself from helping others learn and grow. If you live with a scarcity line of thinking you may hoard your skills out of fear of loss.

Here are some things for you to think about on abundance. How much more giving and service could you do if you were truly abundant? How would it change your life if you started believing there is unlimited abundance of what you need - you just have to ask for it? How much better could your organization be if you stopped hoarding your skills and taught others what you know so they can do better also?

Honesty is being truthful in all that you say and do. If you are honest in your dealings you build trust. With the increase of trust you better your relationships. With the increase in the quality of your relationships your organization becomes stronger.

Here are some things for you to think about on honesty. What has been affected by your honesty or lack of? What has been gained or lost because of it? What can you do to change that? If you gain something great through dishonesty how does that affect you and your relationships with others?

To grow as a leader you must take action. If what you are currently doing is inside your comfort zone then to grow you need to do something outside of that. If you are comfortable talking to people below you but totally uncomfortable talking to people above you then you should work on that. By doing that you expand your abilities and do not stagnate. If you stagnate then you stop growing and if you stop growing your organization stops growing.

Here are some things for you to think about on getting out of your comfort zone. How can you help your organization grow by getting out of your comfort zone? What could you do today to get out of your comfort zone? How would that impact you and those around you?

I challenge you to take action today in becoming the leader you can be.

Debbra Sweet

Entrepreneur, Best Selling Author, Musician, Speaker, Consultant, Coach, Trainer- these are all titles that apply to Sweet Marketing Solutions founder Debbra Sweet.

Exposure to business at an early age and cultivation of artistic talent in music and writing is the background that Debbra Sweet brings to her marketing clients. The unique blend of her endless creativity along with understanding business systems and a great sense of value in client relationships are all key elements that she uses in leading her team of professionals to achieving marketing results for her clients.

Never one to 'wait for things to happen', Debbra opens new doors for her clients and her company in the areas of innovative marketing, advertising and promotions.

Her professional experience on stage as a musician and speaker helps her deliver messages to her clients and ultimately – their clients- in a fresh, inspiring, motivating way. Always focusing on the end results, Debbra helps to streamline the vastness of marketing so her clients can be comfortably involved when they are working towards achieving marketing growth goals.

Contact Debbra Sweet at: www.SweetMarketingSolutions.com and www.DebbraSweet.com or by calling: 888-SWEET-85.

Chapter Three

Step Up To Lead

Debbra Sweet

L eadership is more than stepping into a position that allows you to make decisions for the best interest of others. Leadership involves leading, being able to make decisions, listening, encouraging others and helping others rise up so they too can become leaders.

True leadership also involves a heart to serve. Having a heart to serve either in a personal aspect or in a business arena allows you to give to others while you guide along the way. You give your time, you give your experience. You give your patience and you share your thoughts and insights when it's beneficial to help another person learn, grow and evolve.

There's a statistic that shows in the worldly sense of leadership, only 2% of people are real leaders. Statistics say the rest are followers. I believe that there are many more than 2%- however; these people have never seen themselves through the filter of understanding leadership- so they do not recognize it in themselves. They don't recognize that they already are a leader. I have found that ultimately, the best leaders are those who were initially the best followers.

Leadership is built into every family unit. It's a natural part of who we are as human beings. When we become parents, there is no official guide book that comes along with our children. We lead by trial and error. We learn from others what has worked and what has not. Then we make our own choices to guide our children to help them learn how to make choices and become independent. The cycle then continues.

Even when a traditional family unit is not present, people will bond with others and an unconventional 'family' will develop. From the beginning of time, there has always been a person who is 'in charge' of a family. One person who takes the bulk of responsibility for making choices, educating, sharing, teaching, showing others in that family what to do, where to go and how to do it. Leadership is natural. It's genetically coded into all of us.

Historically, those who are in charge of the family unit then come together and a larger unit of people will bond. These turned into tribes, villages, towns, cities, states and countries. The leaders of the families stepped forward once again- to lead and guide a larger group of people.

If this cycle is so natural and has been around since the beginning of time, then why do so many people today shun, hide or resist the opportunity of leadership? I believe it starts with the perspective of what leadership is. I have met many people who, in their own right, are already great leaders- but they've never thought of themselves as one. They've never recognized that the actions they already take, the choices they already make and the way they interact with people around them- is that of great leadership.

Time to Step Up

I have had the unique opportunity to work with different organizations in a leadership capacity. In these organizations I've stood side by side with people who have had tremendous heart and the inherent ability to step up into a recognized position of leadership. In some cases, everyone thrives, in others, only a select few do- and the difference always comes down to recognizing (or not) ones own ability to lead.

In one organization, the leader whom I was accountable to, spoke about rising leaders from amongst the members of the group and allow them to take on leadership roles. However, he was not willing to honestly look at – or give a chance to -- the other members who were fully capable and willing to serve and lead. He talked about growth through leadership and encouraged everyone to step forth. When there were appropriate times to have others take on leadership roles however, he was unwilling to give them the opportunity. They had the heart and skill sets to lead but they were not confident enough in their abilities to speak up and step up on their own. Those people who wanted to serve didn't recognize the skill sets they had. Their lack of understanding what it takes to lead prevented them from speaking up. Instead they always were just disappointed, unfulfilled followers- privately wanting to be recognized as a leader. This hurt the organization and those individuals.

In another organization which I've been involved with since 1997, called BNI, I have the opportunity to work as a director with business professionals on a weekly basis. One incredible aspect of this organization is that by its very nature it is designed to help develop leaders in the community. Every six months there is an opportunity for professionals to step up into a position of leadership to run a weekly networking meeting. There are three main positions that are needed to oversee the meetings along with support positions that handle a variety of activities.

Every six months, when this changeover occurs, I, as a director of these chapters, have a responsibility to help choose who the next leaders will be. I have a position of leadership to help guide, teach, support and mentor the individuals so they themselves, will guide the other professionals in the chapter to be successful as individual members.

It's an interesting time when the bi-annual change occurs. There are those who willingly jump at the chance to serve and lead. Then there are those who sometimes need to be encouraged to step up. During the six months between this leadership team change over, as their director, I get to observe these members. I see them already acting as a leader- but often, those that need the most encouragement, have not yet seen themselves as one. It's amazing to see the transformation in a person when they first didn't recognize in themselves that they already had the ability to lead, yet they take a chance and step forward. With encouragement, support and training, the personal development that follows is literally life changing. Those people see and feel it- as do those around them.

Not being able to recognize leadership attributes already in operation can unnecessarily prevent people from stepping up from being a proactive, acknowledged leader. As a leader, one of the biggest and most rewarding aspects of leadership, is to help others see it in themselves. When this new perspective happens, magic occurs. The leader and the leader in queue both grow. True leadership is an ongoing cycle of receive, learn, retain and release. We learn as a leader and then we turn around and teach those we are responsible for. They in turn, learn, and then teach those around them.

There are some people who are comfortable with being a leader from an early age. It's just simply who they are. Others are thrown into leadership. They've never really seen themselves acting as a leader and then circumstances arise that put them into the moment where they have to step up. Every person has a choice. When opportunity to lead presents itself- you always have a choice. You can choose to wear the mantle of leadership, or you can choose not to. Chances are if you've been thrown into a circumstance where you are faced with a choice to lead- you already have the foundation of a leader.

The ideal situation for many people is to be given the chance to lead by being asked. When that happens, give yourself acknowledgement. People ask you because they see the leader in you! Your experience up to that point as an active leader may be big – or it may be your first time. Accepting the role can open up learning and growth opportunities for you that will frame your life for years to come.

I remember when I was young; leadership roles were put upon me at an early age. Some of it was natural. I am the oldest of three children and with that is an element of leadership. The younger children in a family typically and instinctually look up to the older sibling to 'show them the ropes'. I was fortunate when I was growing up; there were adults around me who gave me chances to lead. I had not initially seen my own potential, but they did. I recall coaching kids younger than me in a sport I was good at. I remember working with and teaching girls younger than me in the Girl Scouts.

As I grew older and got into junior high and high school, teachers would give me leadership roles. I was very involved in music in school. I had great teachers that led me to excel in music- and then those same teachers turned around and put me into positions to lead my peers with my music skills.

There were times when I resented always being in charge. I didn't always understand why I 'had to be the one in charge'. Many times it seemed like I was the only one who was asked to lead. This may or may not have been the case- but in my perspective, it was reality. People around me always said 'if there was something to be done, Debbra could do it, put her in charge'. What I didn't understand is that I had shown the propensity for leadership from early on and others were seeing it in me before I saw it in myself.

I did recognize however, that at those times, whether the leadership role was handed to me or if I volunteered for it- I always grew. I was able to enjoy moments of great giving. The real reward of my personal growth through leadership was the great satisfaction of seeing that what I did, shared, and taught others around me- helped those people to grow also. Today, when I am asked to lead, I always consider it. Remember, when someone asks you to step up, it's usually because other people have seen the leader within you.

You have value. You have insight. Your experiences are unique- and you can be exactly what those around you need to draw from in order to achieve a mutual goal. Step up the next time there's an opportunity for you to share your leadership. People around you will benefit – and most importantly, you will benefit from within.

John Pol

John Pol is an online business coach who provides mentoring and training to aspiring internet entrepreneurs. He is also the owner of Sole Necessity Shoes and Orthotics, a specialty store specializing in supportive and comfortable footwear and supports.

Projects: Creating and hosting his own television program for educating entrepreneurs on becoming successful leaders and business owners (www.AC-TV.org), teaching students on leveraging the internet and achieving financial success.

- Born and raised in Cincinnati, Ohio
- Youngest of 3 children
- Married, no children
- Bowling Green State University, BA in Visual Communications, BA in Marketing and Business Management.

Websites: www.JohnPol.com
www.GoldmineMarketing.com
www.OnlineProfitSource.com
www.SoleNecessity.com

Email: john@goldminemarketing.com
Phone: 206-338-4393

Chapter Four

Lead With Your Story

John Pol

At the time I am writing this, I am a 25 year old entrepreneur that has only begun to scratch the surface of accomplishments and experiences that will inevitably be my life.

Currently, I am a business owner, consultant, graphic designer, program director/host, coach and student of life. My mission in life is to inspire and empower new leaders, innovators, and influencers for future generations.

I am currently mentoring and coaching individuals to make a full-time income by taking their businesses or business opportunities online. This is where I am right now…at this moment in time…in my life. I am extremely blessed. I have a gorgeous, loving wife, a wonderful family, amazing friends and great relationships.

Let me be the first to tell you that life wasn't always this way. I have endured a great deal in my life before I began having success in business and in life. Let me tell you more about my story…

I am the youngest of 3 children. My parents immigrated here to the United States from Cambodia and Vietnam. I was the first and only born and raised in Cincinnati, Ohio. As a young teen I was very rebellious, got into a lot of trouble, the wrong crowds, crime and drugs. I have been blessed with an extremely loving and amazing mother that helped me get back on the right track. Around age 17, I smartened up, got my act together, my grades together and got into college.

If you're anything like me, then you can probably relate to the fact that I was told my whole life to: "Study hard, get good grades, go to college, get a high-paying job and everything would be just peachy keen".

Well, that didn't exactly turn to out to be great advice.

After graduating college in late 2005 and after experiencing a dozen job interviews, I came to the realization that I am psychologically unemployable. I had no desire to get a 9 to 5 job and retire after working the same job for 40 years… that just wasn't going to happen.

So, I decided to start my own freelance graphic design business. I must say that at first, it was really fantastic. I was making a living from being creative and artistic…I was getting lost in my work!

However, the routine and deadlines quickly got mundane and very stressful. Some weeks I was overwhelmed in work and making money. Other weeks I was pinching pennies with no work at all.

I was easily working 80 hours a week and had no time to enjoy life. I was a one man show! I was the Graphic Designer, the Salesman, the Accountant, the Marketer… you name it, and I did it. This wasn't exactly the "own business" I had envisioned in my mind.

Soon after, I began studying different industries and demographics before beginning my next venture. I soon became very fascinated with the trends and buying habits of the baby boomer industry.

I decided to partner up with a friend that had many years of experience in the specialty footwear industry. There was a huge niche market in my local area of Cincinnati and we decided to go for it. After analyzing the pros and cons of a start-up and a franchise, we decided to create our own brand and create a start-up. I must say that the build out process and the conceptualization of the business was an amazing experience. Looking back I am amazed that we were able to create the business from the mere idea to the grand opening in less than four months.

The business soared in the first 2 years and exceeded our expectations. Our success and credibility grew quite fast in the city of Cincinnati. I was even featured on the cover of the business section of "The Cincinnati Enquirer" as a featured entrepreneur. I was very fortunate to have such a great opportunity and our business soared even more.

After seeing much success I realized that I was falling into many of the same traps that I encountered with my freelance design business. I was a leader in my business, but not in my personal life. I was wearing too many hats and I was working in my business all the time. I was making great money, but I was unable to spend quality time with my family, the ones I love and the ones I was claiming to be working for.

Once again this wasn't exactly the "own business" I had envisioned in my mind. I had created an amazingly successful business, but I felt extremely unfulfilled. I had developed a plan to create a successful business, but I didn't have the end product in mind. I didn't create an exit strategy after the business was up and running.

An extremely important lesson that I had to learn the hard way is that you must always have the end product or end result in mind before you begin to create an action plan.

Dynamic, genuine leadership starts with having the end result clearly envisioned first, and then, work backwards to create a structured action plan. If you fail to do this in your business and in your life, you may be headed into a collision.

In my case, it was an amazing learning experience that I wouldn't change for the world, but I also would not want to experience again. I was coming to the end of one season of my life and entering a new one, one filled with massive potential and abundance.

I took these life lessons and began to search out other options to create the life I wanted. This began the turning point in my life where I first began my journey in the abundant world of the internet. I had been searching around on the internet for ideas for my next business and I ran across a series of videos from a young entrepreneur.

His videos were so powerful that I felt that he was speaking right to me. He spoke of "solo entrepreneurs", leveraging technology, automating your business, and creating a lifestyle by design. This guy was living the life and having the success that I had always dreamed of. So, I contacted this individual and he was surprisingly authentic and genuine. He truly related to my experiences and completely transformed my life.

What do Tiger Woods, Michael Jordan and Tom Brady all have in common?

You give up? They all have great coaches and mentors.

These are teachers to help them embrace their talents and become the absolute best they can be. They have leaders to guide them, to see what they can't see, to direct, support and encourage to be the very best.

I realized that this key factor was what I was missing in my life. He was a leader already and I was willing to be a student. The problem that many self-employed business owners and heads of households have is that they try to do too much work. They aren't leveraging the knowledge of others to help them succeed.

Leverage all 3 of these key elements and you will achieve success beyond your wildest dreams:

1)   The Proper Mindset

2)   Great Coaches & Mentors
3)   Being Part of a Mastermind Community

A mastermind community is a group of like minded entrepreneurs that support each other and help each other achieve great success. These elements will help you become a powerful leader, help you to provide massive value to others, and achieve great success and wealth (in that order).

So, let's tie this all together and let me tell you what I have discovered on my journey to success.

There is one X-Factor in marketing that has been proven successful and has stood the test of time. This X-Factor is "Story Branding". Story Branding is branding you through your unique story, experiences, and personality.

To become a powerful leader and attain success, you must own your feelings, experiences, and your story. You must understand 'The Law of Attraction".

"Success is not to be pursued; it is to be attracted to you by the person you become." -Jim Rohn

Everyone has a unique story to tell. Your unique story has the ability to inspire and empower the lives of countless people. Just like how that young entrepreneur transformed my life and empowered me.

Many people have the desire to become a leader, but are reluctant because they believe that they do not have the skills or that it is just too difficult.

There are going to be certain individuals that will be attracted to you and your story... that won't be attracted to me by John Pol's story.

Do you see how powerful that is?

Everyone has a unique story. Anyone can use their story to brand themselves as a unique leader to help those that will naturally gravitate towards them because of- not in spite of- their story.

Lead with yourself, not your product or business opportunity. People follow people, not products and businesses. When we stop chasing money or time, and start providing value by being our genuine selves, that my friends, is when true success and great leadership opportunities appear.

Regardless of your skills, if you have the desire and passion for success...find you mentor in person, through books, classes or video. Let that mentor and their story help you find the way to discovering your leader within.

Leaders are willing to freely teach others and share from experience.

I must say that all of the programs, e-books, videos, and technology in the world will not guarantee you success. But-if you acquire a proper mindset, mentors, and masterminds, your success as a leader will reach bounds beyond your wildest dreams.

I hope that my story has in some way touched, moved or inspired you to attain greatness in your business career and in your life.

If you would like to discover the "secret" formula that the masses will never know about attaining massive success online... I encourage you to go to one of my websites, send me a message or better yet... give me a call and connect with me!

I look forward to speaking with you and serving as a leader with you soon!

"A leader takes people where they want to go. A great leader takes people where they don't necessarily want to go, but ought to be"

ROSALYNN CARTER

Andy Geldart

Andrew (Andy) Geldart lives Halifax, Nova Scotia with his wife and 2 girls. Andy is active in the community through participation and volunteer work and enjoys traveling, camping and exploring with his family and friends.

Andy also runs the Halifax Academy of the Wei Chin Kung Fu School and takes great pride in teaching and training with those who want to excel in this art. Well being includes training the body and the mind.

Andy is an entrepreneur at heart and developed his own web design business and is involved in the network marketing industry. Through self-development and continued investment in his business, Andy partnered and then co-founded a system which specializes in target marketing for the network marketing industry. This system is designed to train people how to build a solid organization using the power of the Internet.

In addition to developing and working with his network marketing team, Andy plans to develop a larger Kung Fu school which will include a wellness training program.

Web: www.meetandrewj.com
Email: andrew@meetandrewj.com
Kung Fu and Wellness – www.weichin-halifax.org

Chapter Five

Leadership Will Change Your Life

Andy Geldart

"We all want things in life that are on the higher shelves. We can reach those shelves by standing on the books we read." - Jim Rohn.

I magine it just being that easy. All you have to do is read some books and you can change your life.

It couldn't be you say... or could it actually be that easy? Yes it can. Or, it can be as hard as you want.

It is easy. Just like skiing, or playing baseball, or rock climbing, or becoming a physician. Or it can be hard. Just like skiing, or playing baseball, or rock climbing, or becoming a physician.

It's easy like playing guitar and finally learning to get that b-flat while not mixing up your strumming. Another example is learning to ride your bike for the first time, without the training wheels.

It's just as easy to learn to finally tie that reef knot, or jibe without rocking the boat. Or it can be hard, like learning to type, fixing your computer or learning to dive off the 5-metre board.

It is what you make of it. Easy or hard, it is in your head.

Changing your life by reading is just like anything else that you have achieved. You got where you are today by making choices. All you need is choice and the will to want to make it happen. This is the key point. **If you want to make a change in your life, you must change.** You cannot remain the same and simply expect things to change.

"The definition of insanity is doing the same thing over and over

and expecting different results. " - Benjamin Franklin

The ability to change our life is within us all. It is more than simply wanting to make that change. It is a decision. If you do any research on anyone who has ever accomplished anything, they didn't always know how they were going to do it. They just knew they were going to do it.

In terms of where you are right now in your life, take an inventory of all the things around you. Your home, your children, your bike, your family, your stereo; whatever you consider to be important. It could be your bank account, or lack of bank account, your good health or your poor health. If you want to change those things for the better, you must first change the way you think.

If you change the way you think, you will change the way you act. If you change the way you act, you will change your results. By changing your results, you will change your life.

It's called personal development. Leaders are those who are willing to go the extra step – and the first step they take is in developing to become more than who they are today. If you can't help yourself, how can you lead and help others?

Personal Development

How can personal development change your life? Let's look at the journey of personal development and compare it to joining the gym to get in better shape and lose weight.

It's called the "slight edge affect." The slight edge affect is measuring the affects of daily activities over a period of months or years.

Figure 1 outlines how to think of the slight edge affect.

The lesson in this exercise is that all the little things add up.

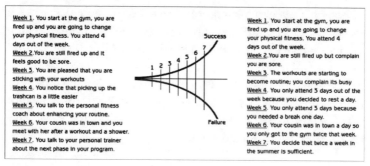

Week 1. You start at the gym, you are fired up and you are going to change your physical fitness. You attend 4 days out of the week.
Week 2. You are still fired up and it feels good to be sore.
Week 3. You are pleased that you are sticking with your workouts
Week 4. You notice that picking up the trashcan is a little easier
Week 5. You talk to the personal fitness coach about enhancing your routine.
Week 6. Your cousin was in town and you meet with her after a workout and a shower.
Week 7. You talk to your personal trainer about the next phase in your program.

Week 1. You start at the gym, you are fired up and you are going to change your physical fitness. You attend 4 days out of the week.
Week 2. You are still fired up but complain you are sore.
Week 3. The workouts are starting to become routine; you complain its busy
Week 4. You only attend 3 days out of the week because you decided to rest a day.
Week 5. You only attend 3 days because you needed a break one day.
Week 6. Your cousin was in town a day so you only got to the gym twice that week.
Week 7. You decide that twice a week in the summer is sufficient.

Figure 1

Repeat this out loud. THE LITTLE THINGS ADD UP. For good or bad, the little things add up. You need to make the choice in which direction you want to go.

Finding your leader within starts with a desire to make a change and then make a commitment to do the little things that will let your leadership skills flourish.

Start your personal development reading routine today and read for 30 minutes. Pick up the same book the next day and read another 30 minutes. Do that same thing every day for 30 - 45 days. Don't look sideways, don't expect results. Don't second-guess what you are doing. Just read every day.

Deciding what to read really depends on what you want to change in your life. I guarantee that what ever you want to change, there is a topic at the bookstore. You can find the perfect mentor to lead and guide you simply by picking books that resonate with you and where you want to go in life.

Personally, I wanted my business to increase. So in order for my business to improve, I had to improve. I started my research and found my way to a book named "Think and Grow Rich" by Napoleon Hill.

Fast forward to today and in less than two years I have read about 20 books. Some I have read two and three times. The number of books I have read is not great by any account, however, how those books have affected my business and more importantly, my life, has had a profound affect.

My personal favourite is "The Success Principles" by Jack Canfield. Other authors I recommend are Jim Rohn, Bob Proctor, Charles, David Schwartz, James Allen, Don Migual Ruiz, Robert Kiyosaki, and Donald Trump.

These are only a small number in a list of dozens of great authors on personal development.

So what does personal development have to do with leadership? The first aspect of leadership is knowing what your limitations are. Reading will teach you about the limitations you never knew you had.

Be the Leader to Develop the Leader

You cannot develop others beyond what they are capable before you experience it yourself. You cannot develop yourself unless you are willing to bring yourself beyond what you are currently capable. Or in other words, you must get out of your comfort zone.

Getting out of your comfort zone is the first phase of becoming a leader.

You must be the leader to develop the leader in yourself. You must start and not be afraid of making mistakes. Learn from those mistakes and learn again. You must learn to change yourself; you must change your thoughts.

Say that again. TO CHANGE YOURSELF, YOU MUST CHANGE YOUR THOUGHTS.

In the next breath say... FEEL THE FEAR AND DO IT ANYWAY.

I started training in the art of Kung Fu at the age of twenty. I earned my black sash some five years later and by the age of twenty-seven I decided I would start teaching. I called my teacher, told him of my intentions and asked for advice so I could start out right. I will never forget those simple words *"No, you must learn as I have, learn by your wits and your training."*

At first I thought it was cold to leave me to make the same mistakes as so many had before me. It took me some time of making mistakes, confusing those whom I taught before I learned exactly what he meant. I had built a small but strong school in those two years, but I had done it myself. I had learned that making mistakes and learning from those mistakes was my leadership development. In order for me teach, I decided I must be prepared to make mistakes. I developed leadership by moving from my comfort zone.

I learned the power of leadership from experience and developed a confidence that has not been shaken since.

When I took stock in my business and realized I must change myself to change my business, I started the path of personal development. After about 40 days of steady reading did I notice the change in results of my business practice. Shortly after, I was taken aside by my business partner and mentor, and was quietly congratulated for the change in my mindset. Only then did I realize I had developed leadership by moving beyond my own limitations. Once again, I developed leadership by moving from my comfort zone.

Upon reflection, I made the parallel between my Kung Fu training and my business training. It is one and the same: to better yourself by changing the way you think. Leadership is within us, some is taught and some we learn.

Action by Decision

It is a decision, plus action in order to achieve your results. To quote a noteworthy phrase, *"Knowledge is Power"*, however, you must apply your knowledge through action for there to be power. To change your attitude, you must change your attitude! For example, instead of watching TV, read a book. Make a decision by removing the negative things or people in your life. Join a different gym. Spend less time at the bars and volunteer at a community center.

Anybody who ever accomplished anything needed to bring themselves beyond their current reality. By reading, and allowing the knowledge and experiences of others to guide and lead you, you will start to face those limitations you never knew you had.

Once you move beyond and defeat a limitation, move out of your comfort zone and complete a task or assignment, you will gain a confidence you never knew you had. Then the most amazing thing will happen. You will do it again... and again. Once you feel the power of accomplishment, keep reading and keep improving for that will teach you more. Keep feeling the fear and doing it anyway. There will always be fear. The way to defeat fear is through action.

"I don't run away from a challenge because I am afraid. Instead, I run toward it because the only way to escape fear is to trample it beneath your feet" – Nadai Comaneci.

To Your Success!

Section 2:

Inspiration and Instruction in Leadership

Pam Russell

Pam Russell has over 30 years of experience in Business Development, Sales and Marketing, with a strong background in the IT Industry where she had a very successful career as a Systems Analyst, an Account Manager and a Program Manager.

She is the owner of The Full Potential, a marketing services company, specializing in creative solutions for client relations management, including many marketing tactics such as promotional marketing products, SendOutCards (a follow up and contact system for business and personal needs), and custom client relations strategic plans.

Pam obtained her Bachelor's Degree in Linguistics from the University of Maryland and her MBA from the University of Phoenix. Her personal affiliations include Business Network International (BNI), Women in Business (WIB), American Mensa, Tall Clubs International and Alpha Chi Omega.

www.thefullpotential.com
Office: 858-592-0663
Cell: 619-823-7615
pam@thefullpotential.com

Chapter Six

Be the Leader You Were Born to Be

Pam Russell

Growing up as a military dependent taught me some amazing life lessons. I learned how to make friends quickly and how to maintain them for life. I learned how to pack everything from clothes to dishes, from books to furniture.

I learned that a home is not just some house filled with furniture—any apartment or house or building will do, as long as Mom and Dad and my sister and brother were there. "Home is where your heart is," my mother would tell us, "as long as we are all there together, that place will be our home." Life lessons were learned as we traveled from Texas to Austria, from Michigan to Pakistan, from Washington, D.C. to Germany.

All the lessons I learned have helped to shape the person I am today: the values I hold dear, the personality I have, the people I choose to love. But the lesson that has had perhaps the most impact on my business life and the careers I have chosen, was the lesson about leadership.

I had many leadership role models throughout my childhood: my Dad, my Mom, my Sunday school teacher, our pastor, and my teachers (Mrs. Latimer and Mr. Hay especially), the assistant principal, and so many more. Early on, I didn't really understand the true meaning of the word "leader". Rather, I had the belief that all these people were there to tell me what to do.

This confusion is one that many people have upon entering the business world. In business, depending on our chosen profession, we are confronted with different categories of what we believe to be our "leaders". They are our supervisors, the Master Sergeant, the "boss," the Vice President of a company, our manager. Early on I believed that every one of these "authority" figures was actually a "leader."

But life was to teach me a great lesson: the difference between a "boss" or "manager" (or whatever title they may have had) and a true "leader." The person who helped me to recognize this difference and embrace it for myself was one of the people I believed was there to tell me what to do - my Dad.

Dad was a military officer, an Infantryman and a master para-trooper. He had fought in World War II, been a member of the OSS, would eventually be a Special Forces Green Beret and would advise troops in South Vietnam. I saw him as the head of our family. He was tough, with a commanding presence, and I loved him completely! All Dad had to do was to say "I am disappointed in you," and I would do anything I could to please him!

After I left home and entered the business world, I found myself at times emulating my Dad in the business world. I was tough, decisive, a hard worker, excellent at whatever I did. I considered myself to be a good "leader." Little did I know that I was not considered a leader at all - I was considered a good, competent employee, with good "management" potential. But I had yet to understand the characteristics that I needed to develop in order for people to want to FOLLOW me! That would come later, after I had climbed my way through a number of business successes.

I remember after I had received a great promotion and went "home" to visit with my parents. I was speaking with my Dad and we were discussing my frustration with my apparent inability to get the people on my team to go along with some of my ideas. I knew that my ideas were the right way to go - I even had the endorsement of my senior VP - but for some reason I was having difficulty with my staff members. I felt as if they were working against me.

Dad listened as I shared my frustrations with him that day, and then he asked me an important question. "Are you **telling** your people what you want them to do or are you **showing** them the way?"

I was really confused by this, and it took Dad a while to get me to understand. What I had been doing was telling my people the right way to do things - the way I always did them. I was not earning their respect; I was not leading the way. I was under the impression that if I knew the right way to do something and told my people how to do it, then that meant I was a good leader. Was I ever wrong!

The reality is that people are motivated by people who show them the way, who guide them, who demonstrate the best techniques.

Employees - especially mine - did not believe that I cared about them. Although I was really good at doing my job, I was lousy at motivating people to follow me. Once I grasped this difference, it opened up my life to a new way of being. It also has helped me understand that every person I meet, in fact, every person I don't meet, has the potential to be a leader to someone about something! We all have those people in our lives who will continue to tell us what to do. They are the "bosses." But each of us has the inherent potential to be a leader.

Think about the examples in your own life. If you are a parent, you have the potential to be a great leader in your family. You can guide, set the example, and demonstrate through your own actions exactly how you would like your children to behave. How many of us have seen parents who yell or scream directions at their children ("don't smoke", "don't drink", "don't do drugs") and yet, the behavior they demonstrate is contrary to their directions (they smoke, drink, AND do drugs!)? They are not leaders. They are bullies and the children they raise will struggle through their lives with these mixed messages: directions or directives in direct contradiction with the examples they observe.

On the other hand, have you ever seen parents with children

seem to constantly be doing all the right things? These parents demonstrate—on a daily basis—the behaviors and the attitudes they want their children to have. They guide, they set great examples, they lead their children, and they set a great precedence for their children.

Another example would be a committee on which you are a member. It could be a committee at your church, at work, a social group to which you belong, a parents' group for your children (PTA, Soccer League, etc.), or even a Neighborhood Watch Group or a Homeowner's Association. Each of these groups provide the members with the opportunity to demonstrate their leadership potential. Are you more inclined to listen to and follow the suggestions of someone who sets a great example, or the person who tries to dictate to everyone?

As I reflect back on that conversation with my Dad, I realize what I great gift he had given me. As my father, he had always demonstrated a positive attitude, care for others, love for the family, pride in one's achievements, doing the best job possible, striving for excellence. And those were the same qualities I had developed in myself! Dad was my very first true "leader!"

Who are the people who have been the leaders in YOUR life? And are you a leader to someone? Who do you guide, show the way to, encourage, and set an example for? Each of us has at least one leader within us - it is up to us to bring that forth and share ourselves with others.

"You do not lead by hitting people over the head - that's assault, not leadership."

Dwight D. Eisenhower

Carol Wooden Groark

Carol is a fun-loving educator, wife and mother of three. She lives with her husband, Bob, and children, Michael, Matthew and Mikayla on Long Island, NY. Carol is an incentive trip earner, and top recruiter and leader with Discovery Toys.

You can reach her at:

Phone: 631-771-2030
Email: carolstoystore@optonline.net
www.discoverytoyslink.com/carolgroark

Chapter Seven

Leadership - Why not you? Why not NOW?

Carol Wooden Groark

Have you ever wondered what the secret formula is to all of those people that have made it to the top of their company or in their personal life? How do they all get to become so successful and you are still struggling to make ends meet and get that next promotion? Well, there is no real secret.

The choice is actually yours because everyone has the ability to get up that ladder to success and become a leader in their own right. You just have to make up your mind to do it now. One of my favorite quotes by Og Mandino is, *"I will persist until I succeed"*.

You need to have a Never Give Up philosophy and have a Positive Mental Attitude in all aspects of your life in order to come out on top. Babe Ruth struck out many more times than you'd think in order to become the Home Run Record-holder. He didn't just quit because he had lots of strike outs. He knew he'd get up again and the more times he got up at bat, the better the chance to hit another home run.

Babe Ruth's persistence led the way to inspire thousands for years. How one perceives a situation is going to affect the final outcome. You must take the approach that every failure is a learning experience and once you begin to do this, you will become a successful leader.

A little background on my first influential mentor when I began my work-from-home business, my grandmother, Ruth Krier. She not only successfully raised seven children after her abusive husband left them, but she always put her family's needs first.

She was an independent woman that worked outside the home and she never once complained because she made her children, her WHY. As her children grew and she retired, she went to live with them and her 27 grandchildren and eventually some of her 14 great grandchildren.

She would always lend a hand with chores and errands and most importantly encouraged each one of us to not be followers of other people's dreams and to go after our dreams and make them come true. She said, "Don't listen to those that make fun of you. Stand on your own two feet and just keep going no matter what."

When I started out in my business, there were plenty of negative comments from those that were trying to "help" me not make the big mistake of thinking I would become successful. They would say: 'Maybe I should go to college or get a "real" job.' Grandma just pulled me aside and said, "I know you'll do just fine and I know you will be the only one out of them all that will be most successful. Keep up the great job and never, ever give up on yourself and your dreams." At that point, I knew I had to keep going. My family deserved that chance. I deserved that chance, and I made the decision to really go after it all.

You need to make a decision to decide. I decided that my children are my WHY. They are why I get up a little earlier in the morning and stay up a little later after they are in bed at night. They are why I WILL make it to the TOP of Discovery Toys in the next two years. They are why I was a top recruiter last year. They are why I have the courage to lead my team to success. They are why I don't attend every social and school function, but I'm at almost every game or concert they perform in.

I want them to be able to have every opportunity to be able to choose for themselves what they want in life. I lead by example and don't settle for the minimum, but go way beyond. I play full out and expect them to dream big and aim higher than they think is possible. Why settle for mediocrity and complacency when there is a rich and rewarding future within your grasp?

Invest in your business. Invest in your life. This is where you need to make choices that will help you get your business or life to the next level. I plan out my day, spend time to reflect on my accomplishments and have my goals and dreams where I can see them when I first get up and right before I go to sleep at night. Spend quality time with your family while they are there. Enjoy every moment. Life is too precious to look back and say, "If only I had…."

I sometimes go out of state to work my business and take my entire family with me. My business allows us this convenience and opportunity to include them in our fulfillment of dreams and goals. They learn more by being with you, if schedules allow. They get to watch and hear your successes and they will model you. They look up to you and will thank you as they grow into leaders, too.

Feed your mind with plenty of personal growth and development. Seek out your mentors that you have been reading and learning from in your business and life studies. Do you have an inspirational friend, manager or colleague that is at the top of their game? Are there any seminars or trainings you would like to attend? Then you need to be there! Be willing to travel to learn from the best.

I was very fortunate that I was pointed toward my Diamond National Sales Director's training that she was having halfway across the country two years ago. I seized that opportunity and took my then 11 year-old son with me. WOW! We attended the session and it forever changed our lives for the better. We participated in separate group activities and Michael even helped his team come up with a name, slogan and song.

We learned many helpful things for my business and it helped me become an even better mom, wife and team leader. My son learned so much more than he will in school at this one event. This has proven to be just the beginning of my successful journey and it's not about to slow down anytime soon. Learning lessons can be anywhere – and leadership inspiration can even come from a child.

While on your journey to successes you must continue to build your library with only the best books, CD's, DVD's and training materials. Turn your car into a rolling classroom and attend everything your company has to offer, like seminars and conventions. You just might learn more at your company's conventions in 2 days than you will learn in 2 years had you not attended.

Make a commitment to your team and family. Show them that they can be successful, too. Be there for the people in your life. Hold conference calls and lead them on the call with answers to their questions. Get involved with people in the community. Encourage them to ask even more questions and be sure they understand the answers. Find out what their "why's" are and where they want to go with their business and their life.

Everybody has different visions and goals. If they don't know exactly where they want to be and what their goals are, it's your job as their leader to help guide them to find their goals and help them create a plan to achieve them.

Make the choice to build your fabulous future starting right now. What are you waiting for? You alone are in control of what path your life will take and you are the only one that can make that decision to decide.

My grandmother's belief in me, along with my director's training and encouragement to help me decide to take on this successful journey to the top with my family will be forever in the forefront of my mind.

I encourage you to become the leader I know that is inside each of you. I believe in you. I am on my way to the TOP! Why not you? Why not NOW?

"I start with the premise that the function of leadership is to produce more leaders, not more followers."

Ralph Nader

Courtney Walsh

Courtney A. Walsh is an experienced blogger, communications professional, freelance writer, adventurer, author and mental wellness speaker.

With an extensive background in marketing, advertising, creative writing and cultural studies, Walsh has worked with the U.S. National Park Service and on a project for MTV's Real World. Recently, she completed a memoir, "Lipstick and Thongs in the Loony Bin", and was on the Fox network's Morning show with Mike and Juliet: www.youtube.com/courtneyawalsh

www.courtneyawalsh.com
www.scribechickie.blogspot.com
www.lipstickandthongbook.com

Chapter Eight

Following Your Inner Compass to Leadership

Courtney Walsh

"Real isn't how you are made, it's a thing that happens to you."
~from the Velveteen Rabbit

Growing up--my dad, a high-level educator, had all the leadership books of the greats: Napoleon Hill, Dale Carnegie, Stephen Covey etc., littered around our house. These books clogged the stairs, were strewn about casually on coffee tables and spilled out from magazine racks. I came to know leadership and success principles by osmosis. I was surrounded by these jaunty pictures of smiling men in suits whose very essence seemed to shout from the pages with tireless encouragement about thinking big and being bold.

My mom was one of a dying breed... in the days before the term "stay-at-home mom" or even "homemaker" she was of the old-school variety 'housewife' and 'mother' and she embraced and executed those roles beautifully. Over the years, she'd add artist, interior decorator and grandmother to her repertoire. Home was her office, her queendom and her arena to play with success. For her, successful leadership could mean a day with few sibling squabbles, the clean dinner dishes put away and nodding off gently in front of Masterpiece Theater.

None of these books, (in the 70's or 80's anyway) had women on the covers. Nowadays we have so many strong, business-oriented, female role model offerings: Suze Orman, Oprah, Hillary and Louise Hay to name a few. I can honestly say that my journey with success and leadership has had very little to do with any of the people on the covers or in the pages of these success books, but everything to do with the learning that was acquired directly from the people in my own life: teachers, aunts, uncles, my parents, grandparents and even TV characters. But more important than any lessons that any of these people imparted....

my greatest teacher, the one I owe the most to, including my life... is FAILURE.

Every time I failed in my early life, my heart broke open a bit and let in some light. Each failure gave me the freedom and permission to pick myself up and try again in a different way. If I lost a job, a relationship ended or a dream died, I learned. From ALL of my failures came my greatest successes. The greatest leaders of modern day often have many failures along the way.

Now I simply look for the lesson in the failure as if it were not merely the silver lining... but the whole point. This goes beyond making lemonade or looking on the bright side. It's more than enduring rejection or building character or any of that other stuff people told me along the way. I learned from the wins and the gold stars and the back pats and the A's as well. They were shiny, they felt good, but ultimately were fleeting and sometimes even empty. I had to tune into my own inner compass and let it steer me in the direction of my dreams.

Understanding leadership in my life started by taking myself and the very concept of failure and success with humor, grace, and huge grains of salt and allowing myself to learn from each circumstance and opportunity that came about because of my choices.

One of these "failed" dreams was moving to San Diego from Boston. A New England girl born-and-bred, I often recalled being about three years old, sitting on my dad's lap in the car in our driveway and pretending to steer the wheel.

"Where to, Courtney?" my dad would ask... *"We can go anywhere you like."*

"CALIFORN-JAH DADDY, CALIFORN-JAH!" I'd burst his eardrums with my enthusiasm for this sunny place I imagined far away. In my mind I saw a place with nothing but blue skies, endless ocean and the sun winking playfully over all. (Even at

three I felt that snow was overrated.)

Fast forward to twenty years later, I'd graduated college, lived and studied in Spain and was now ready to move to "Californ-jah". I packed up my meager belongings and moved out there. No job, no car, very little savings. I was going to become a screenwriter. I had a gleam in my eye, a dream in my heart and a ton of hope… but no real PLAN.

A few weeks into my stay I was still looking for a job and had come to realize that my new roommate and her boyfriend were going through a VERY messy breakup. I felt completely caught in the middle and ended up calling 911 when her beau threw my trunk down three flights of stairs in a fit of rage because she was leaving him. (Not exactly my vision of a shiny, happy place.) More like a nightmare come true. So I tucked my tail between my legs and moved home after a month of drama, dwindling money and ever dimming hope.

Life had zapped me into a new level of understanding of what my once alcoholic grandfather had meant when he used to say, *"Life is hard and I'm soft."* But grandpa got clean and then helped hundreds of others onto the path of sobriety, too. He was a success story of an unconventional kind of leadership. Unintentionally, he was an example of leadership in my life. An example of making a choice to lead one's own life and overcoming hardships then turning around to help others.

I tried to chalk my time in California up to bad timing, lack of planning, naiveté, etc. I just couldn't make my dream fit my memories behind the steering wheel no matter how hard I tried. Finally, out of money, out of faith and out of the blue I got the sudden realization, *"I don't have to cling to a dream I had when I was three. My life is not a fairy tale or a fantasy, but it is MINE. I can just go home and start again."* In that moment I stepped up a bit to redirect and lead my own life.

When I was 27, I had another brush with failure. It was during a meeting my well-intentioned father had set up for me with one of his influential friends who had millions of dollars and was supposedly a patron of the arts. I was going to talk to him about my writing. It was an enlightening experience.

Waiting 35 minutes to meet with the self-made Real Estate mogul in the plush downtown office, I shuffled through papers wondering what I was doing there. Seeking information, advice, something, anything. The receptionist outside his office door was recounting her drunken birthday weekend, gum-smacking loudly, acrylic nails tapping on the keyboard, giggling into her space-age headset phone.

Receptionist: *"So then Johnny and Mike were brawling in the middle of the street. I know can you believe those jerks?"* Tap-tap, chew-chew. Finally I spoke with my fathers friend. In his office were the obligatory family photos. Ski-trip to beach. All seasons covered.

"How did you get your start?" I asked timidly.

MBA from Stanford... a chance meeting with the governor. I imagined two men locked in a staring contest assessing each other; a kind of unspoken playground dare.

After explaining to him that a screenplay I'd been on the verge of optioning was now, ahem, available again for potential producers (since the woman who was going to make my film had suddenly gone bankrupt) his response was what I thought of as typically corporate.

"Deals fall through all the time. Try advertising- more stability."

Some of his other helpful gems: *"Some of my friends are heroes... artistes, freelance writers, novelists."* (Slight condescension in the faux French accented "arteeste.") he'd advised distractedly. *"But it's tough to make any kind of decent living in that field. Take any kind of foot-in-the-door job.*"

He pushed some papers around. He was an A.D.H.D. night-mare. Eyes darting everywhere and then, mercifully, he took a phone call. After a brusque conversation with the person on the other end of the phone, I worked up my nerve a bit.

A few more questions lobbed, followed by awkward, time-stopped silence. I thanked him, shook his hand... mine shaking so badly that the pumping motion was almost unnecessary, I left deflated and confused, a cavern of overwhelming exhaustion opening up inside me.

On the train ride home after the meeting, my mind replayed the scene again. The floodgates of absurdity of asking a real estate mogul for career advice as a writer hit me.

Disembarking from the train I walked home in a haze. A friend tried to soothe my existential angst: "*Doesn't know you... hasn't read your work... middle-aged business guy... Don't let it get you down...*"

Other phrases I'd heard over the years echoed in my head: "*We all have to grow up sometime. How will you pay your bills? You're so talented... You can do your writing thing on the side.*" (A career a la carte?) "*Follow your dream. Marry rich. Nature of networking- sometimes you win, sometimes you lose.*"

On the way home, I stopped at the drugstore, bought a soda, looking under the cap... some marketing contest ploy? It said: "*Sorry... please try again.*"

And again and again. Who knew if I was born to be a writer or not and, in the meantime, I'd travel and gather material for stories, stretch my horizons beyond their limits, fall in love, get my heart shredded a few times and keep on persevering. I'd take day jobs and night jobs and third shift jobs. The clock would be a friend, an enemy and a neutral observer all the while.

I began to realize that you need to have a vision, a plan and then find the right mentor to successfully guide your dream, help you navigate it downstream and show you the ropes. There's a lot of winging it and stumbling and then picking yourself up again in the process.

I kept writing. I lived paycheck to paycheck for years, yet I'd write on the side, for me and for an invisible audience of readers that might someday connect with my words. I knew it wouldn't be easy. But I knew that's what real success was. It starts with personal leadership. It continues with trying new ideas and failing and learning and growing and changing and trusting. And then doing it all over again.

Today, I enjoy fruits of success that came out of my early learning through risks and failures. Those challenges forced me to see things a different way. I persevered, overcame and discovered how to lead my life using my inner compass in order to achieve my dreams and passions.

I'm still learning every day. Now I take these life stories and lessons and share them with others. It's leadership through learning that puts you on the road to success in your life. And believing in yourself no matter what.

*"Your thoughts are the seeds
for your words and deeds."*

R. Frank Tulak

Kim Hughes

Kim Hughes is the author of ***The FIRST Real Estate Virtual Assistant Handbook*** and is the co-founder of the International Real Estate Assistant Association (www.IREAA.com). She is a speaker on several real estate panels throughout the real estate industry and has been a highly sought after real estate virtual assistant on many levels.

She has achieved success on several levels during her career in the real estate industry. She currently has a successful real estate virtual assistant company and has expanded to offer her knowledge and experience to coach/mentor those that would like to achieve their goals as a virtual assistant.

Kim is a Wife, Mother, Real Estate Virtual Assistant and a Virtual Assistant Coach. She resides in East Texas with her husband Paul, her children and her 4 dogs and 3 cats. She enjoys traveling, reading, scrapbooking and helping others achieve their dreams.

Kim Hughes
Kim@KimHughes.com
www.KimHughes.com
www.YourVirtualAssistantCoach.com

Chapter Nine

Leadership Roles and Believing in Yourself

Kim Hughes

There are two initial sides to being a leader. One side is leading a group as a whole. The other is leading individuals who contribute to the larger group. As a leader in business or for a personal endeavor, keeping a clear perspective of the many types of personalities you might have to support and lead is important.

In business you lead yourself, your staff, your employees, sometimes even your vendors and suppliers. On a personal level, leadership can involve managing many people and even many roles for the greater good.

Understanding that each of the people you are responsible for may need to be lead in a different way is a secret to great leadership. This eventually allows others to rise up and some day lead as well. There are many ways to motivate, speak, communicate and educate the people you lead. Taking the time to identify the nuances of the individuals in the group around you and relating that to your leadership style is priceless.

Believing In Yourself

The one thing I have learned in all my years as an employee in Corporate America and as a self-employed virtual assistant is that no matter what obstacles you face, as long as you have the strong desire and the determination you can achieve your dreams. But, you first need to believe in yourself.

Your ideas can become reality. If I let all the obstacles guide me I would not be where I am today. When I began my business as a virtual assistant there were only a hand full of VAs and the concept was not well known. On top of that I only knew real estate. For me to be successful I decided to only specialize in real estate. I became a Real Estate Virtual Assistant. The term was not well known and those that had heard of one were not sure of the concept.

But, I knew this is exactly what I wanted and because of my strong desire to build my own company and to work from home, I knew I had to do this. The financial need was there, my desire was strong and my determination was off the charts. Because of these three things and by staying focused and working hard I was able to succeed. I helped to create a new concept among the virtual assistant industry. Unknowingly I was becoming a leader in un-chartered territory. Need, desire and determination are important elements in discovering your ability to be a leader.

If you have the same desire to own your own company or step into leadership in an area of your life, but not sure what to offer in the way of services then I recommend that you first start off with a resume- or taking personal inventory of your strengths and attributes. Create this resume/personal profile sheet as if you were applying for the job of the century, which you are. The only difference is that you will be the boss.

Once you have completed the resume have someone read it to give you an honest opinion and then revise it. This will be your platform of what services you will offer your clients and it will showcase areas in which you will be a great fit for leadership. When you write your resume and personal inventory sheet, you will see where your strengths are and where there is opportunity to still grow.

What ever your business, you need to be proficient in basic skill sets. As a leader, your personal profile sheet should also identify what skill sets you have in that area. You will need to know how to work with details, creating policy and procedures for your business. Leaders often have to be able to not only look at the big picture but also understand the relevance of details that others may bring forth to support that larger vision.

Know Your Audience

As a role model in business - regardless of the market or

location of your services - to be most successful you need to always know your audience. You should know what expectations have been set from your audience. Are they looking for you to lead by example? Are they looking to be taught how to do things for themselves? Do they expect you to be outgoing, dynamic and a great orator- or is the quiet leader, the staid, confident, succinctly spoken type better for your group?

Sometimes as a leader you will be working as if everything is needed yesterday and time is of the essence. You need to be prepared for any type of a situation. There may be decisions you will need to make that are urgent. Other times you will see that you have the ability to slow down your decisions and allow time to be on your side. You will teach others by simply allowing them to see you take the lead.

There's a good chance you are already practicing these skills. As a business professional or as an individual, you have to determine every day what decisions and actions are the real priority.

Managing your expectations of your capabilities and then managing the expectations of those around you will allow you to lead with confidence. Look at what you do now. Can you see areas where this is already mastered?

Review each request or question from your team and tell them what they can expect from your time involvement and when they will hear back from you. Communicate these expectations quickly. Do not ever leave them guessing.

Get to know the audience you will lead as quickly as possible to understand their personality, work habits and communication style. Doing so makes sure what you are doing for them is understood by them. They are part of your team, part of the bigger picture.

Being able to be clearly communicate to them in a way that they understand is another area great leaders excel. Do you have a chance to practice this in your life today? If so, take it. Make an effort to knowingly communicate in a way that others will relate to. See how it makes a difference in the outcomes you need or want.

If you are unfamiliar with different ways you can communicate with others then educate yourself! There are many great resources available now to help you interact with people around you that will avoid confusion, conflict and hurt feelings. It is possible to change how you act and speak with others. The more you put forth effort to do this, the leader within in you will develop quickly and your audience will respond to you with greater loyalty and willingness to work with you.

We are all human and no one is perfect by any means, but you have a responsibility to provide the best communication possible to each and every person you deal with. If you do not understand a request, procedure or task that you need to accomplish, find your mentor and talk to them. Be sure they communicate with you also in a way that you can quickly comprehend what you need to do. The best leaders acknowledge that they may not know everything themselves but they know who to go to in order to get the information that they need.

Always, always stay a step ahead of your team members. Attention to details and good communication skills (both in speaking and listening) will allow you to do this. This is what makes a true leader so valuable.

The ones you lead expect you to bring creative, fresh and unique ideas to the table for them. Don't wait for them to ask for simple ideas, learn from other leaders to see what works for them and offer it to all those you lead. Sharing ideas is part of what genuine leaders offer.

Leadership Ethics

We have heard of 'leaders' in the world that lead everyone only one way. There are cases where these so called leaders have achieved some of their vision- but often it is through fear, intimidation and trepidation inflicted upon those around them. That is not the type of leadership we are talking about here. It is about serving those around you.

Run your business and your leadership position on high standards with your morals and values in place. By striving to be the best in your field, you will earn the right to say you're the best!

Continue to Grow

True leaders are always ready to take on new roles of leadership and learn along the way. They keep integrity from within strong and will use the ability to tie in the big picture with details. This skill takes time to refine- but it is worth it.

Your desire to be a leader is a journey. There is always growth along the way. You will find that the roles you take on as a leader will be different today from what they were in the past. They will be different in the future as well. Enjoy the journey as you find your own leadership style!

Fran McCully

Fran McCully holds a degree in Business Administration from the University of Idaho and has over 25 years of combined experience in administrative and executive assistance, finance and budgeting, and in general business with experience gained from years of employment at Washington State University.

Her business *Your Administrative Solutions* specializes in bookkeeping and accounting, database and business-plan development, and human resource services.

Your Administrative Solutions
www.youradministrativesolutions.com
208-877-1736 Office
208-301-0325 Cell
fran@youradministrativesolutions.com

Chapter Ten

The Growth of Virtual Independence

Fran McCully

As I prepared to write this article, I thought about how many life experiences had contributed to my becoming a leader-personally and in my business. People had trusted my knowledge, depended on my abilities, and respected my judgment. And I liked that. I also valued being my own person and making my own way. So, four years ago when I entered the world of the self-employed entrepreneur, I knew that my strong work ethic and solid skill base would prove invaluable as I stepped into another strategic leadership position; this time in the fast-growing world of virtual assistants.

Preparing the Ground

As the youngest of three and the only girl, I grew up in Southern California in an area called La Sierra. Our parents raised us in a very strict Catholic environment. When I told my parents that I planned to attend college, they enthusiastically supported the idea. I would be the first generation in my family to go to college, and my mother had always planned that I would attend a local, Catholic university.

I had yearnings of a bigger dream inside me. I wasn't sure about the details, but I knew that I would be taking a different direction than what my family was expecting. Not in their wildest dreams, did they ever think that I would leave home, much less leave the area! My dream, however, was to venture out to the wilderness.

I didn't choose a college by what it offered as far as academics but rather by how remote it was! I wanted out of the big city. I chose to go to the University of Idaho in Moscow, Idaho.

Needless to say, my parents and friends, especially my high

school sweetheart, thought I had lost my mind! I knew better. High school graduation arrived. I enjoyed my last summer in California, going to the beach, having fun! And then, I packed.

Planting the Seed

Late summer arrived and so did my trip to Idaho. With all of my belongings stuffed into my VW Bug, I set off on my journey. I will never forget my father and mother waving goodbye as I pulled out of the driveway. I still could not believe that my father was allowing me to take this journey—on my own—with no adult supervision! I had made my first step in following through on a decision to lead my own life.

I arrived at the University of Idaho a week later to find a loving, small-town atmosphere. It didn't take me long to settle in, find lots of friends, and begin my adventure. It felt good. It felt right. At the end of the first semester, however, my high school sweetheart realized I was not going to come back to California, so he joined me in Idaho.

We married and moved to a small town called Troy, about eight miles from Moscow. I continued to attend classes at the U of I and our family grew by two; one girl and one boy. Unfortunately, our lives began to change. We grew apart and divorce loomed on the horizon. I found myself needing to take lead in the direction of where my life and my children's would go from here.

Waiting for Signs of Life

Since getting married, I became a stay-at-home Mom taking just a few classes at the U of I. Now, I realized that I would have to go to work as a single mom. Fortunately, I was able to find a job at the hospital in Pullman; unfortunately, it didn't last long. A back injury laid me up for the next three years.

During that time, I lived on disability payments and learned what it was to live from month to month with very little money. After two back surgeries, the pain had disappeared only to return six months later. This time, they diagnosed fibromyalgia. Another decision to be made here. Become a victim or continue to lead my life by example. I chose to continue.

By now, Idaho's workman's comp office decided to send me to school to be retrained instead of sending me more disability checks. I went on to finish my education. I had a year to go to complete my degree in Business Administration and Management. Slowly, I gathered the tools I needed to move me toward a more secure independence. As a single mom my internal drive to be independent helped me to continue to build upon the skill sets I already had while showing my children how to be an achiever in any situation.

Seeing it Sprout

My goal in life at that time was to obtain work at Washington State University (WSU) in Pullman; an ideal job complete with benefits and insurance. I was sure it did not get any better than that. I had heard, however, that WSU did not hire just anyone. It was very hard to get in. Although I had overcome and achieved much already in my life, I didn't have a champion in my corner really encouraging me to go for it. I didn't see at that time that my leadership skills were already well developed.

So, with a diploma and very little confidence, I passed on applying at WSU and instead found a job at Northwestern Mutual Life Insurance Company in Pullman. I ended up working at the insurance company for three years thinking I didn't have enough experience to move in the big world of WSU. Then it happened; the insurance company closed its doors.

Fortunately, during those three years I had grown to realize that I really did have the skills and the ability to lead my family and myself in wise decisions for providing our livelihood. Now I had a second chance to go for my dream job. I could not pass this opportunity twice!

Northwestern laid me off on a Friday, WSU interviewed me on the following Monday, and they hired me the next Wednesday. I didn't even have a chance to open a claim at the unemployment office! I could hardly believe that I was set with my dream job.

With two children at my side, I began my 20-year career at WSU. People always said once you get in at WSU, you are in for life. How very true. The college provided a solid base of knowledge and experience that would serve me well. Yet those deep yearnings for something more kept worming their way around in my mind. I just wished I knew what they were really about!

Nurturing the New Growth

Throughout the years, I grew professionally but personally I had only dated occasionally. It never seemed to really work. Either my kids hated him or he did not like my kids.

When my daughter was in high school, I began to think that I would never remarry or have a significant other. Then, one of the girls in my office started pestering me to go out with her father-in-law. "He is just like you", she would say; "Go out on a date; you would get along famously." I never took her seriously, though. I just couldn't see it happening.

One day, however, just to get her to leave me alone, I agreed to meet him; but, I warned her not to get her hopes up. We went on our first date on April 12, 1997, were together as a couple by 1998, and were married soon after. So much for not getting serious!

One of his favorite stories to tell people is how I would jump out of the car when we pulled into my driveway. I had to get inside the door as fast as I could before he attempted to kiss me because I knew in my heart that once that happened, it would be all over with.

Adding More Sunlight

Soon, my life in the small town of Moscow ended; and we moved to Deary, Idaho, and started our life on his property. We started our life together in his very small, tacky trailer; a situation both of us knew would not fly for long.

We began building our dream home in the winter of 1998 and moved into our beautiful log home in 2001. We built this 3900 square foot home on our own, putting up each log ourselves. The only outside assistance we had was a plumber and an electrician. All the while, that little kernel of an idea and a bigger dream continued to grow. What would it be when it grew up?

About this time, I began what I call my mid-life crisis. I realized that during much of my life I had had not one to depend on except myself. I had raised my children without help from their father, earned a degree, found employment, and made a home for my family. Yet, somewhere inside, I had sheltered a desire to be an entrepreneur, to start my own business. Questions started budding in my mind. What business would I start? How could I manage? Where would I be?

Meanwhile, I began doing the bookkeeping for my husband's newly acquired business, a wild, land firefighting business where he would contract with the forest service to fight these fires. I quickly became an expert using QuickBooks and processing government contracts for the business. Could this be a seed of an idea for my own business? But, how? The notion still lay just beyond my grasp.

Watching It Grow

Meanwhile, I had become the Executive Assistant to the Director of the WWAMI Program. This joint project was created to assist first-year medical students, designing curriculum and coordinating classes for students on both the Idaho and

Washington campuses.

During regularly-held meetings with my four staff members, I liked to include some stimulating activities to boost morale and increase motivation. I asked each person to come to the meetings with an innovative idea to share. One day, a staff member discussed this new concept that was becoming quite popular among stay-at-home moms, early retirees, or mid-lifers. I listened attentively as she defined this intriguing concept she called the virtual assistant industry.

A Virtual Assistant (VA), she informed us, acted as an independent entrepreneur providing administrative, creative and/or technical services. Utilizing advanced technological modes of communication and data delivery, a professional VA assists clients in his/her area of expertise from his/her own office on a contractual basis. She proceeded to tell us about the set-up one would need to start this business.

The light bulb lit up; it even glowed. As she spoke, my mind reeled. I had it all—the equipment, the knowledge, and the expertise necessary to start this business!! At that point, I finally new what that yearning was for- to be an independent business owner. I had everything except the clients.

The following week, I retired from WSU, and six months later, I was sitting in my log home ready and waiting for business to come along. I had taken that large step to tie in all of my life experiences and I saw the leader really within myself. Your Administrative Solutions was born in 2004.

Reaping the Harvest

Fast forward three years. I have a small but successful Virtual Assistant company where I support clients worldwide, virtually.

The majority of my clients are in other parts of the United States.

I call myself a virtual professional and QuickBooks expert who partners with small business owners, micro companies, solopreneurs, and individuals to reduce their workload, grow their business, and boost their profits—all the while saving them money. I specialize in bookkeeping, human resource services, and database development and maintenance.

Each day, my confidence and leadership grows. I meet people online, at conferences, in networking groups, and through referrals. My business continues to expand and develop. And, to think it all started with a tiny seed nurtured by life itself.

What can your life "grow" for you? Tap into your life resources, cultivate your own abilities, and transplant them into your dream world. Let the leader in you find the light and blossom.

"Time is neutral and does not change things. With courage and initiative, leaders change things."

Jesse Jackson

Section 3:

Personal Insights to Becoming a Leader

Ed Mercer

Being an entrepreneur Mr. Mercer has owned several of his own businesses taking them to the top of their field. A self made millionaire by age 27, he has amassed an incredible repertoire of achievement, including working around the world and helping 35 other people become millionaires.

Mr. Mercer has shared the stage with some of the most accomplished speakers in the world such as Bob Proctor, Mark Victor Hansen, Jack Canfield, T. Harv Eker, Deepak Chopra, John Gray, Lisa Nichols, Jay Abraham, Bob Circosta, Armand Moran and Ron Heagy.

As the largest private developer in Costa Rica, Mr. Mercer and his wife amassed over 6000 acres of breathtaking land and created a One-Stop-Shop facility for North Americans. He is an active philanthropist and member of Habit for Humanity, National Geographic, The World Wildlife Fund, Greenpeace and many other similar organizations. He has set his targets to give back and help the community around him. His greatest personal achievement is the founding of "The Edward R. Mercer Foundation" which is dedicated to the betterment of the planet through ecological conservation and education.

www.EdMercer.com
www.MercerFoundation.com

Chapter Eleven

Unwavering Integrity

Ed Mercer

In determining what it is that defines success and failure in a person, many often wonder: Is it a gene? The lifestyle we grew up with? Was there a pivotal point in our childhood, or for that matter, our adulthood? Were the planets lined up at the certain time of our birth? For many, it is seemingly impossible to say. But for me, I have come to understand an unfailing formula.

My experience has shown that all kinds of people, from all different cultures, lifestyles and ages have become exceptionally successful. We are in a league of men and women who caught the dream and will never let go, or perhaps can't let go. We all persevere to reach our goal no matter what... and confidently succeed. On this journey, and from my 50+ years experience as an entrepreneur, it is an honor to share with each of you my own interpretation of the 'formula' for exceptional success and great leadership.

There are many important elements I could elaborate on. Elements such as: passion, commitment, discipline, vision, clarity and drive. Each of these qualities is worthy and necessary. However, as we are referring to *complete* success as a leader, here I will share with you the qualities that I believe one must first embody. The first is integrity, and in my opinion no others truly count.

According to Webster's Dictionary definition, Integrity is: *an undivided or unbroken completeness. Integrity is the basing of one's actions on an internally consistent framework of principles. Relevant views of wholeness may also emphasize commitment and authenticity. Integrity can be seen as a virtue in that accountability and moral responsibility are often indicated as necessary tools for maintaining consistency between one's actions and one's principles, methods and measures.*

From my experience, I have come to understand that integrity is the true foundational quality that leadership is built upon – a common ingredient for most success formulas. The greatest qualities in a leader are strengthened and supported by integrity.

Successful people, whether they are Millionaires or even Billionaires, are not extraordinary people; they are simply people who accomplish extraordinary tasks. Tasks which require an extraordinary amount of teamwork and passion, which must be tied together with unfaltering integrity, otherwise your team or project will not have the determination and persistence to survive.

In hindsight, I sometimes wonder where my own principles of success stem from. I was a street person at the age of 15, always looked at and considered as a pathetic loser. My clothes were from the Salvation Army and I was 100 pounds of skin and bones. Parents would not allow their children to associate with me; saying that poverty might be contagious and that I would ultimately end up in prison. My Grandfather, who raised me, said the only reason they make desks so small in grade 4 is so that you won't fit into them when you're 25. Thus, the only thing that kept me from going to a University was High School.

I gathered that my lack of education provided me with the vehicle that allowed me to not know enough to let the continual putdowns and criticisms get to me, but rather use them as a source of motivation, proving to everyone they were wrong about me. With very little education, I chose to get my degree from the school of life. I established my own Board of Directors: Henry Ford, Charles M. Schwab, John F. Rockefeller, Thomas Edison, Dale Carnegie, Napoleon Hill and many, many others. Although they did not know they were on my board, their influence in my businesses and personal life was profound.

I read hundreds of books and listened to thousands of hours of audios on successful people, realizing the only reason they write books on these types of people is because they don't have a "loser" section in the library. I found the common denominator of all successful people and great leaders is a willingness to do things that failures won't do. As well as this, I found a profound sense of integrity permeated throughout all of their successes.

Integrity is a core value in the leaders who are revered throughout time. It was inspiration and having identified these traits from my board of directors and more, that allowed me to ultimately go on to become a millionaire by the age of 27. And yes, I do have some eerie sense of satisfaction knowing that I proved everyone wrong, because I simply can't imagine where I'd be had I listened to them.

Although I didn't realize it at the time, I began a life-long decision to be exceptionally successful. However, in order to be a winner or to be successful, you have to surround yourself with positive ideas and thoughts. Thoughts can rule your life – negative or positive. You are what you watch, read, and allow into your life, thusly becoming a product of your environment. Show me your friends and I'll show you your future.

As I have told all of my associates, integrity builds credibility. It only takes one lie to taint your entire credibility and from there it's all down hill. We move in and out of a fast pace life with thousands of options and you really only have one chance to win someone over. Whether it is a client, a business associate, a friend or family member, what you do and say in any situation will reflect on your integrity's scorecard. This means that you can't justify an action in one situation while hypocritically doing the opposite in another. It just doesn't work in the long term.

Speaking of long term, it took me twenty years to become an overnight success. I have found that another by-product of this fast pace world is that many will do and say anything to "make the deal". This just doesn't work! Oh sure, you'll make a quick buck, but you sacrificed your integrity for the long term to do it. That's where the beginning of the end starts, because eventually it will catch up to you and your name, business and personal life will suffer the decay.

You will have your integrity attacked on many occasions. Why? Generally because the weak minded have no where else to go. It seems when things are running fine and all is going good, someone's jealousy will zero in on you and say "You don't deserve this and I will do my best to make sure you don't get it".

They will poke and prod at your business ethics and then your life, looking for a weakness. Many times they don't find anything and that's when they go for the jugular. They attack your personal values and beliefs.

In times like this, I say never fear the criticism, people are going to criticize you no matter what, live with it. Don't fall into their trap, because criticism is a disease of the weak minded. You see this most commonly with sports figures and celebrities, constantly being bombarded by those who are jealous of their success and feel the need to attack it on some level, just to insert some kind of value into their own empty lives.

If these people could simply remove jealousy from their lives, they would find an incredible world out there waiting for them, yourself as well. If you are doing the right things and moving forward in the right direction, there is no need to be jealous of anyone. Instead, use the envy you're feeling as a motivator to move yourself in the direction you are attracted towards. Otherwise, the jealousy will destroy your dreams from the inside out.

I remember when an associate asked me my opinion on whether or not he should tell a lie to another associate, as a means to protect a project. I told him he had two choices; the first, was to go through with the lie and know that he has jeopardized his personal and professional integrity. The second, was to tell the truth and know that he did the right thing, even though there may have been a short term consequence. He chose the later.

To summarize; never leave your mind open to the negative influence of others. You have 100% control of only one thing; your thoughts. Remember, success and great leadership is no more than a state of mind.

Here's a simple test; if you had a best friend, would you want it to be you? If the answer is no, you have a lot of work to do. If you do not love, respect or trust yourself, no one else will. If you're not happy inside, you will not be happy outside and people will see you as you see yourself. You are the only person that can make a difference in your life. When you make decisions in your life based on integrity, you will make a great difference in the lives of others.

Do not walk in front of me; I may not follow. Do not walk behind me; I may not lead. But walk beside me, and be my friend. Follow your heart wherever it takes you and be happy, for life is brief and very fragile, only loaned to us for a little while.

Bardi Toto

Bardi Toto, a single mom of two, burnt out nurse of 14 years. Went from living paycheck to paycheck to earning over $200k her first 8 months on the internet with NO prior Experience at all!

Bardi was raised with a poverty mindset, coming from a broken home where she lost her mother to alcohol at age 15. Beating the odds she overcame adversity, turned the labels given to her, along with the many fears and excuses she had, into pure success. Bardi inspires and empowers others to stop making excuses and live the life of freedom they deserve. She is publishing her first CD "Living a Life of Freedom, Not Excuses," which was inspired by her mentor Dani Johnson. Bardi wants to share the lessons of her life and help people find the leader and the power they really have within themselves. "Taking Action" and "Being Real" is her motto and she defiantly lives by it.

To find out more go to:

www.whoisbardi.com
www.DESTINEDTOSUCCESS.COM
www.youtube.com/topmarketingguru
www.myspace.com/empoweringguru

Chapter Twelve

Living a Life of Freedom, Not Excuses

Bardi Toto

E very person on this planet has a dream, a wish, things and situations they strongly desire. But a dream, we believe is just a dream, something out of reach, beyond our grasp. Is it any wonder we don't have the slightest clue of how, or in fact **if**, we can bring those dreams, wishes, and desires into our reality? We all want to have great things however we are not creating the outcome that we want. We complain we don't have enough money, we don't have the success we want, the relationship we want, the happiness we want and it is all because we have settled for less in our lives.

Each one of us has it within to do and be the leader and achieve everything we desire. We need to pull that out of ourselves and wake up the person that we were intended to be, that we were meant to be. In order to get what you want you must first know what you want and have the end in view.

For a long time I was stuck in this phase because of the verbal abuse I received as a child. How could I know what I wanted when I was told I would never finish what I started, I would never amount to anything and I would fail at whatever I did. People cannot see the outcome of their dreams because they are stuck in this phase. I had a fear of failure and a fear of success.

I had a mother who told me everyday we couldn't afford this or that, and how poor we were, but we moved to Hawaii when I was 13. Talk about mixed signals! I got my first job at 14 at a florist because I thought we were so poor and I ended up lying to get the job to help my mother. Come to find out we were wealthy; she hoarded money and spent my college trust fund that was left to me by my grandparents. Talk about a formula for disaster!

I sabotaged myself in every way for success based on my beliefs. I know there are those reading this that do not have my story but you have experienced some situation that has made you feel as though you cannot even dream. Those dreams you have experienced are out of reach and so far fetched, and I am here to tell you they are not. If I can do it, you can do it!

"Try and fail, but don't fail to try."
- Stephen Kaggwa

"Some men see things as they are and say why?
I dream of things that never were and say why not?"
-George Bernard Shaw

DREAM BIG

When I decided on October 30, 2006 I was done with nursing I was not sure what I was going to do. I knew I was finished. I was over worked, under paid, saw and experienced things in the nursing field that I knew were absolutely wrong. My intension to be a nurse was to help others and make a change in family's lives, not suck all the money out of families and give pills, surgeries and procedures they did not need.

I sat there for 2 months until one day I received a call from an old friend. This friend had been in every program on the internet; however, he was the only one I knew that had ever succeeded. Bob had a mindset like nobody I had ever met and the best part is that he believed in me.

Parallel to my nursing I started a marketing company on the internet in 1997. I had gotten ripped off by a company and decided I was going to do it myself. I had a dream, woke up at 3 am, went downstairs and wrote an ad about my company from the point as if it already existed. It was an overnight success and I had more work than I could handle. I advertised for over 200 companies out there including Amway, Life Force, Alpine and Nu Skin just to name a few.

When Bob approached me in October 2006 he told me he was in a new program and how he knew I could "make bank" as he put it. He told me "you are a go-getter," a leader, and the elite 2%. He saw in me what I did not see in myself. He told me "I know you will succeed." I had advertised for all these programs but had never been in one. I had seen so many people fail, not because of my marketing but because of their mindset, and their excuses.

Looking back after going to my First Steps to Success with Dani Johnson in Dallas Texas, March 2008, I realized why I attracted people that made excuses and why they failed. I was at that time in my life living a life of Excuses; I attracted people who made excuses.

Although I was successful I still made excuses why I was not going to get into a program. The excuse I would tell people is that "it was a conflict of interest owning a marketing company," and "I need to focus on my marketing." To be honest I was scared to death! I was told I would fail at everything in my life, so why try, and why dream?

January 3, 2007 I called Bob and wished him a Happy New Year. The first thing he asked was "What happened to you?", and I blurted out I was scared. He informs me he made $35,000 between November and December. I didn't know who I was more mad at, myself or at him! I was so angry I told my excuses to go to you know where!

I got on the internet with this program and did $18,000 my first 21 days, $60,000 my first 45 days and $200,000 my first 8 months. It blew my mind because I decided to start Living as a Leader, a Life of Freedom and not Excuses. Excuses lead to depression, stress and health problems. No wonder I had thyroid problems!

Before starting this venture on the internet, I watched the movie "The Secret" on January 29, 2007; I then wrote my self a check for $100,000 and wrote my intention down on paper. I learned from Dani and others you don't compromise when you write down your goals. This year my goal is a million and I will do it.

I live a life of urgency everyday and you can too. Remember I am the woman who was verbally abused, was told I could never do anything right and that I would fail at everything I tried. I am the same woman who had $67,000 and my identity stolen from me over night in 2005 and ended up at the State assistance office the next morning. Look at me now. I live a life of freedom, not excuses.

GOALS WILL MAKE YOU GROW- BECOME A LEADER

Give yourself permission to DREAM BIG. The biggest reward I have received is not the materialistic things but about whom I have become through pursuing my dreams. The investments I have made in myself; for example: a First Steps Seminar, reading books, listening to CDS over and over, learning how to outsource by hiring people who knew how to do things better than myself. At one point I thought I could do everything and had no trust for someone else to help me.

As I grew on the internet I had to learn how to balance my work and my family life. I am a "Ruby" according to Dani Johnson, so my Time management skills were out the window. It wasn't until March 2008 that I really learned time management through First Steps to Success.

With my success I have experienced loss and I am sure you have seen that as well. The man who took $67,000 from me over night and stole my identity took my faith, self esteem and trust in mankind but he did not take my skills. Who I was and what I had learned throughout the years, all the skills I developed- he could not take away and nobody ever can.

Remember you are the author of your own story and your life is a story! You are a LEADER and you might not even know it, because you have not given yourself that permission. You have not stopped living a life of excuses. Write down your own ending and make it happen! Take Action instead of making excuses. How did I learn a life of urgency? It was not over night and very hard.

I live a life of urgency everyday but there are days I struggle. Nobody ever said it would be easy. Here is a scenario and an exercise you can do. First, if we had no fear of rejection and we knew we would not fail, what would be some of the things we would do?

Take yourself back to age 5, when you had that mindset of a persistent child; when you would ask for anything and do everything without fear of rejection. What Happened? You can change this and lead. Write Down Your Dreams and Goals.

As you reach your Goals cross them off your list as if you were going shopping. Write the sentence "I did it" or "SUCCESS" so that your mind receives the signal. It is a true achievement. Look at your list when you may be feeling down or discouraged because we all get that way sometimes. Be re-inspired by your achievements. I never could see my accomplishments because I never wrote them down. People would rant and rave about what I had done but because of that negative mentality I had, I thought they were no big deal.

When I finally wrote down my accomplishments, I discovered I had accomplished a lot. Two Bachelors Degrees, a Nursing Degree, being an inventor, skydiving 3 times over the North Shore of Oahu, owning a Health Store in Tonga. I traveled all over, buying houses on my own as a single mom being dependent on nobody, doing things people dream of doing.

If I never had taken that first step none of these things would have happened.

Once you are clear about what you want, you turn Your Dreams into Goals and Objectives. Turn your dream list into a measurable objective. For instance: I will weigh 120 lbs by July 24, 2008, not I want to lose weight. Saying I want to lose weight is a vague want and is not specific. As Dani says *"Nothing can become Dynamic until it becomes Specific."*

You must take each and every part of your vision and turn it into an objective. Make a comprehensive list. Once you have done this, you are ready to go on to the step of turning your dreams into a reality and becoming the Leader you were born to be.

Remember I overcame adversity, labels, and I beat the odds. I stopped making excuses and started living a life of freedom. I became the leader I was meant to be, and you can too! Remember Your Income follows your personal growth. Your personal Growth determines whether or not you work hard. Believe in yourself, write down your dreams and make them a reality.

"The very essence of leadership is that you have to have a vision."

Theodore Hesburgh

Hillary Jollimore

Hillary Jollimore is a creative business and marketing professional with a passion for writing and an even stronger passion
for learning. She is a leading expert on anger and stress reduc-
tion and has authored many workshops, including the Mall Parking Lot Theory and Serenity Through Stress.

Hillary is a dynamic and engaging speaker and coach. She has
broadened her small circle of mentees and will be offering Stress
Elimination seminars and workshops after the release of her book
on the subject in September/October of 2008. She currently offers private and group workshops on an as scheduled basis.

Hillary can be reached at hillary@alexispromotions.com, 813-
903-9803 or through her website at www.hillaryjollimore.com.

Photo by Dan Casey www.pixcasey.com

Chapter Thirteen

The Stress Elimination Solution: True Leadership from a Serene Mind

Hillary Jollimore

We used to play a game called True Colors™ and during this game, friends would assemble and vote for the others in the group with certain characteristics. I always won the categories like, person whose life is most like a soap opera, drama queen, most likely to implode and just about anything else that represented teenage angst.

The biggest problem with this was that it continued well into my thirties! While my friends and peers were moving on to bigger and better things, I was becoming bigger, but not necessarily a better person.

In The Beginning

There was always something wrong with me. There was always an excuse why I couldn't fix what was wrong. There was always stress, generally followed by anger, gradually followed by depression and a never ending search for an answer. I was positive it had to be something physiological. So, I muddled through much of my youth, using whatever means I could find to drown out the thundering mess which had become my life.

The lack of control I exhibited stifled me in more ways than I ever could have known. As talented and capable as I knew I was, I was never in a position of authority in business or in friendships. I was always the follower and always trying to please the leader. Allowing others to take credit for my work and my ideas, actually handing them their tickets forward, I held myself back for fear of screwing something up and for fear of not being liked. I worried all of the time. I got angry a lot and I never moved forward.

The Awakening

Then one day I heard something called the serenity prayer. It is a simple verse written by a Protestant theologian by the name of Reinhold Neibuhr circa 1934. It goes like this: "God, give us the grace to accept with serenity the things that cannot be changed, courage to change the things that should be changed, and the wisdom to know one from the other."

It made me realize that not only could stress and anger be "managed", they could be, for the most part, eliminated. I set out on a journey to find out just how to do that. Once I figured it out, I knew I had to share it.

I realized that there were things out of my control and there were really things I could change. Here was the realization that if I knew the difference, I could calmly take charge of my life and my destination. The realization that all that I wanted to achieve, I could easily have and be- if I learned, nay, taught myself how to think a bit differently. I learned to control my thoughts instead of my thoughts controlling me. I learned to lead my outcomes by being proactive in my thoughts instead of reactive to my situation.

It's actually pretty simple. It's very contagious. It's like parking at the mall. It goes like this: When I go to the mall, I park in the first available space. I walk from the car to the store. I take time to enjoy being outside. I admire the different rims on all of the different cars. I enjoy the variety of paint colors on all of the cars. I smile at people walking and driving by me and wave to those who make eye contact. If, by chance, it's raining, I inhale the sweet smell of the falling rain whilst strolling under my umbrella.

I hold the door open for those coming in with me and those exiting with small children and packages. I use all of those basic manners taught to me by my parents oh so many years ago. The process is amazing. Most people in this situation are not used to being in contact with someone who genuinely wants to give a positive moment to their life. The people around me transform as they thank me, or return my "pardon me" as we narrowly miss each other in the crowded isles. The minimum wage checkout people return smiles and begin to enjoy the moment rather than dreaming of a beer after work or stressing over bills.

With my calm serenity and my refusal to give in to the mundane stressors of the day, I have not only conserved my energy for more constructive endeavors, I lead those around me, even those who have had only the slightest interaction with me, into a better place. During this process, I discovered that it's all about the little things and all about the moment. Those little things and those moments, those are the things that gather momentum exponentially. Those are the things that form our emotions, our thought patterns, our relationships and ultimately, our destiny.

With my new approach and attitude I discovered something. Suddenly I was no longer the follower. I was the leader! I was the calm rational person everyone turned to. I was the force. What a difference this has made in my life! The best part is knowing that not only was I in control of my own life, but that I could show this process to others and they could use it to develop their untapped leadership potential.

The Process

The first thing I had to learn before I could make any real changes was to abandon many of my perceptions. I had to understand the difference between the important and the menial in order to sort them apart. At the end, I had a much better idea of what I not only wanted to accomplish in my life, but what I needed to do so I could enjoy the time God gave me.

Realization number one was a pretty amazing one. Little children, even the kindest of them, are quite self-centered. They have no concept of a world without them. They see life as the here and the now and just the here and the now that they are in.

They know how to enjoy the moment for what it is.

As we grow older we become aware of the world around us. We like to think we are informed. This information allows us to worry about things like traffic and global warming. We anticipate things in the future that we have no control over. We regret and/or long for the things in the past. That is a huge burden to put on oneself!

That burden causes stress. Releasing that burden can eliminate stress. What a concept that is! Once that stressor is removed, just imagine what that energy can be put toward. Just imagine what can be accomplished.

I decided that 99% of the burdens I carried around were unnecessary and that 1% I needed to keep could be handled with a bit of help from a higher power. My elimination list began. I started with some of the most obvious things I could think of.

I started with traffic – I used to be one of those drivers who had to be first to get somewhere. I don't know where I was going that risking my life was not as important as that extra thirty seconds I would gain by passing the panel van, but it must have been something. Traffic happens and it happens worse because of people who drive like I did.

How do I eliminate stress from traffic? I have to go to work. I have to get places. It started by changing my perspective and then creating a plan to allow me more time to arrive safely at my destinations and enjoy the ride a long the way. (The more I engaged in releasing stress around the little things, the more time in my life I had to live happily and with enjoyment.) Breakthrough! Yes, that one statement was the key to all of it.

That 99% of stress, wanting something, feeling like something has to be done right away or feeling like everything has to be fixed now ... I had spent so much time worrying about what has to be done now to either make up for lost time yesterday or get to ready for tomorrow that I had forgotten how to enjoy being in the moment now. I'd be willing to bet there are many people who feel the same way.

The Solution

The solution took some time and some effort to implement. Once I had it in place I realized that there was much more to it than fixing myself. I had to reach out to the people closest to me and show them how to implement the solution to a more serene life. I had to show them, by leading with example how changing their perspective would benefit them. That way, I would be constantly reinforced by the positive energy all around me. It all goes back to being contagious. I didn't want to allow the stress to contaminate me again so I had to get away from it.

I wanted to play True ColorsTM and be voted "unflappable" and finally, I was able to do just that. No more drama queen with a soap opera life. That girl had figured out a way to exert some control over her life. Yes, I figured out how to eliminate the stress.

Well, that was the beginning. Today, I enjoy the now. I am not careless with my obligations for tomorrow. I just plan properly for them so that there is no stress involved. My relationships are better with my husband, parents, children, family and friends. My career has no boundaries. The possibilities seem endless.

Yesterday I had lunch with a very young friend of mine. She was planning on making a career change and wasn't sure how to go about a few of the steps. We talked for three hours. We drew communication diagrams. I tried to bring out all that she had to offer. When I got home I had an email from her:

"I just wanted to say that you truly inspire me! Lunch was great, thanks again. It's nice to finally talk to someone who's smart AND motivated. Anyway thanks for the advice, I put in my two weeks notice and Rich shook my hand like he was proud of me".

To do that for one person gives me so much to be grateful for. My workshops and writings allow me to share with so many others and it is truly a blessing. I built the foundation of stress and anger elimination for myself to change my life. It did, and now I am leading the way to share it with the world.

"Leaders aren't born they are made. And they are made just like anything else, through hard work. And that's the price we'll have to pay to achieve that goal, or any goal."

Vince Lombardi

Jason Purifie

Minister Jason Purifie aka JPX performed as a dancer for a premier rap group. He quickly advanced to emcee. He served as Vice-President in the highly ranked Scott Bulldogs of Toledo, Ohio.

JPX has released several music albums from multiple record labels before giving his life to the Lord and becoming a Christian minister. JPX is dedicated to the Street Ministry serving the Kingdom by saving Souls in the hood.

Min Jason L. Purifie
Grace Temple C.O.G.I.C.
Owner Sevenge Musick Publishing
Artist JPX 357
MM. Amazon lodge #4
R.A.M.. Maumee Chapter #6

Phone: 419-320-0863
Email: sevengemusick@gmail.com
www.myspace.com/jptheunknown

Chapter Fourteen

Leadership Through Conviction and Belief in a Higher Power

Jason Purifie

W hen I was given the opportunity to write this chapter I realized that I have never written in this format. So I prayed that I would be given what to say that would help the reader. I had to go to the Lord to ask for guidance. And that's when it hit me. I can say with out a doubt it has been me going to the Lord for direction, with whole hearted conviction and belief, which has got me to where I am in my life. This conviction and focused belief in a bigger vision has sculpted me into the leader I am today so that I can inspire others.

It was my faith in the Lord and being obedient to the Holy Spirit that moved me in ways unimagined. I want to say it was me, all the way, but that would be wrong. I can only take credit for reading the word and believing that His plan for me was better than the one I had. The truth is a good leader is great follower first. I chose to be a great follower of Christ.

I have had to depend on the Word more than a few times. I love music and because of my experiences as a dancer and a performer, I can tell you the music business is full snakes and enemies both seen and unseen. From the beginning to the end there seems to be somebody ready to take advantage of you or misdirect you for their gain at every turn.

It makes no difference whether it's secular or non secular; people are people and you have to learn to watch at all times. I was fortunate to know my worth and I was able to see skill level and evaluate the cost of doing business. Early on I learned that I had to lead my own life with wise choices so as to not get taken advantage of. (Not placing my pearls in front of swine meant something to me.) When I realized that too often, it was indeed the case of people wanting to take advantage of me, I moved on as soon as I could.

Why should you give away something that means so much, (my integrity, talent, and respect for my self and my music) to someone that doesn't respect those values? Another precious choice to be watchful of is our time. At the end of the day we all have the same amount of time. How will you choose to spend yours?

Because I am an artist I have to spend time practicing. I have to perfect my craft or who would want to see it or hear it! If I gave a halfway performance would you want to hear that? No I don't think so.

It's the same in business and in life. You have to work at it to get it right. There are always going to be times when you mess up and miss the mark. Not everything you do will be right. And that's okay. As long as you learn from the experience and grow you'll always be going forward.

The moment you stop learning I guarantee you're headed in the wrong direction. Those who desire to find the leader within – and then step up to engage it, always need to be willing to make a commitment to learn.

When you think you already know everything, your conviction and belief is in yourself and yourself only. This is also the basis of pride. Remember pride comes before the fall, and when you're trying to get to the top and pride gets in the way, a fall is going to hurt. If you have fallen – or do fall in the future, look for the lesson in the failure. Leadership means being able to honestly look at ourselves first- before we can effectively lead others.

The road to leadership isn't always given to the swift but to he that endures. Patience. Endurance. Stamina. All are qualities of a good leader. You have to have patience to work with people because not everybody works and learns the same. If a person is committed to your cause they will rise to the task you ask. Their commitment to grow and follow you will help them along. You may have to encourage them but you can definitely work with a committed person. But it does take patience.

Endurance is necessary because great leadership doesn't happen overnight. The first door may not open right away and you may have to knock on 99 doors before the right opportunity for your style of leadership opens. If you quit at 98 the world you're trying to get to, to lead, to share, to inspire, will never know you because you quit.

The thing you learn at door 98 may be what prepared you for 99, and when your door for opportunity opens- that's where the stamina comes in. Because at the end of the day you have to be able to keep the race going.

Now that you've arrived as a leader, you have to be able to have the wherewithal to do you whatever it is you do best. Can you imagine if after Jesus got to the cross- what life would be like if he didn't have the stamina to go through with it? Or if he got down off the cross saying "I'm too tired for this." Where would we be?

It's the same with us today. The bumps and bruises and life lessons along the way prepare us for what we are called to do. We develop wisdom to lead our own lives. That wisdom can then lead others. The stamina we develop as we learn to lead is for after we have arrived. Are you willing to in the race to become a great leader in your life?

I guarantee if you do it God's way, you will receive blessings ten fold. I have never seen the righteous forsaken or their seed begging bread.

When I switched from secular to the non secular world of living and thoughts, I still had to do music. It has taken me sometime to figure a way to be relevant and entertaining with out comprising the integrity of what I was called to do. I had to steward my talents and make wise decisions so I could deliver product that would help reach out and lead others.

When I started I was spending hundreds of dollars in the studio away from home and paying for a product that was not where it needed to be. I began moving the studio engineer out of the way so I could save time in getting my product to acceptable standards.

I learned he was making his money buy the hour and was concerned about the quality of my product. His greed was in the way and I had a problem with that. I was thankful that technology today has leveled the playing field. I didn't have to stay on that path of lack of someone else's integrity for too long. I made a choice to change my circumstances and lead myself in a better direction that would support my hearts passion.

I took a job at Guitar Center and from the time the store opened till the day I left I was top salesmen every month. I won so much gear I eventually had all the pieces for my own studio and I didn't have do anything but my job.

When that position ended abruptly I was shocked and a bit hurt, but as I walked away I noticed that my time there had been the vehicle I needed to get me where I'm going. That was door 98.

I persevered with my conviction and belief in a higher power to lead me in the right direction. I got up again and continued knocking. I went to God. I believe the Lord's Prayer. As a matter of fact, that's all I pray. (Kiss theory. Keep It Simple Stupid.) I ask his will be done, and he gives me the desires of my heart. Not everything that I want but the things that are good according to his purpose for me.

For I had long said I would like to work for myself. At every company I had been at I was the top dog. I always said if I could do this for this company why couldn't I do it for myself? I sold over $670,000 worth of gear for Guitar Center and I only made like $29,000 myself that year. I didn't like the split. Nor the disrespect for my pearls (i.e.: my time).

I've always been in management and I've always been in sales but music is what I love. I had a job to pay for music and now here was the perfect opportunity to do what I love and get paid doing it. Is that not true success?

As I look back it was certain steps along the way that lead to this. These life lessons created the foothold and the platform that pre-pared me to be a great leader for others. I remember following the still voice within saying "now step out".

Things had lined up for me to be in a position to do my own thing. I had what I needed to do it. I had the experience and the talent. I learned in these previous situations valuable lessons- and one of the biggest is the importance of having rock solid belief in yourself and being able to follow a higher power. In order to continue to lead, you have to continue to learn. Then, you need to be willing to teach others.

It's not about how much you make it's about how much you keep. And to keep more than I used to make doing what I was destined to do allows me the ability to tell you what I've learned.

As a leader you will have to follow sometimes but make sure the one you follow is Christ. Even though at times you may find yourself in a bad spot don't give up. The trip is not over. Take what you can from it and keep moving. The journey is the ex-perience and that experience is what will make you the leader you are going to be.

Ed Badrak

Ed Badrak - His gift is the ability to identify and develop niche marketing opportunities. He ran insurance agencies, taking his agency to be one of the 10 top agencies in the company for 3 years running. After 11 years in insurance he ran and owned a mortgage company.

In addition to business, Badrak served on the national boards for three entertainment labor unions helping to preserve performers' rights. He was also actively involved in educating people about the importance of helping veterans to return to civilian life after service to our nation.

Because he appreciates market trends, Ed is currently building a successful MLM business using the people skills he has developed over the past 30 years. His passion is helping developing entrepreneurs to find their niche for success.

To find out more about him and his speaking events visit his website at www.badrak.net

Phone: 619-857-4422
Email: ed@badrak.net

Chapter Fifteen

Humor Anyone?

Ed Badrak

Leadership

"Responsible for individuals and their actions" -- what an ominous statement; a little scary, yet that is the blessing and scourge because a joyful moment can go terribly wrong in an instant. How you respond will determine the overall experience for everyone affiliated with you.

Most people relate leadership to a job, yet leadership traverses service organizations, Labor unions, theater, business, parenting and, of course, you. The greatest challenge is learning to lead yourself to success. Personal leadership is paramount to you being effective in anything you do. You need to understand why you are doing something because success does not always result in a financial gain. Emotional satisfaction is frequently what makes you tick.

Questions For My Readers

How do you help an individual achieve success? How do you delegate a task? How do you follow up with an individual? How do you inspire people to achieve their personal greatness? Here are a few ideas, which are peppered with several stories of how I've dealt with situations. Enjoy.

My First Time

The first time I was put in charge of people I was in the military. It was not by choice, skill or aptitude; it just happened. I was the most senior-ranked person by 48 hours and one of the youngest people in the section. The orders from my officer in charge were to not mess up.

I figured the older guys were going to eat me alive when they found out I was in charge, but they ended up betting on how long I would last. I wanted to take part in that wager, but they would not let me because they thought I would throw the job to win the bet. Little did they know that my ego was in full gear and I was determined to survive. I was not sure how to survive while not getting my clock cleaned in the process.

Not knowing what to do I took the wager sheet and asked every person whose date had passed to give me a chance and asked them what they were willing to do so our life together would be easier. None of the requests were out of line, and there was one in particular that has stuck with me all these years.

One sailor who was a lot older and bigger than I, he admitted to me that he had a hard time reading. Every day, when out of sight of everyone, we worked on his learning how to read and use the library. After about six months he drilled enough and had the confidence to pass the test for the next rank. The greatest compliment I could have received was he decided to get his G.E.D. and he stopped calling me "college boy."

The result was I survived not because of my military rank but by getting everyone to willingly show up to work on time, do their job right the first time, and learn how to not be caught if they were going to goof off. My first lesson was finding success in mutual goals. Rank and title did not mean success in doing the job; it was how I treated the people who reported to me. Having that success, I still could not buy a good conduct ribbon with six years of service.

Embrace The Opportunity To Lead

I have found that as soon as you become the leader you seize the job with enthusiasm whether you became the man for it on purpose, or by default. Do yourself a favor, be gracious and do not say you do not want to be the leader. Whether the command comes from respect, talent or skill, it elicits a special emotion from those who come into contact with you if you are the go-to person, so behave with class.

There was a time while running an insurance agency I made a hard decision to lay off a sizable portion of my sales staff. After completing a training conference on goals, I took a long look in the mirror and, as my father would say, "If you don't like what you see in the mirror, change it."

The old rule of 20% of the organization did the work while the other 80% were drinking my coffee applied to my agency. I liked all of them, I had moved up the industry ladder with these people, and this was not going to be easy yet it was my responsibility to help them move on to a different career. Their non-production on the job indicated to me that they were not going to change. Agency production standards were not being met, and in some instances neither were their basic financial needs.

When I presented the plan to my sales managers' to change the environment they were not on board with my decision. We had a lengthy managers meeting off-site wherein I met with each manager and reviewed each of their agent's records to determine if we had met all of our responsibilities in fulfilling an intra-dependant entrepreneurial relationship between the independent contractors and the agency.

I asked each manager about their goals and desires and asked them to evaluate me so I would be more effective in supporting them. There was resentment from a few managers, because in their opinion things were fine the way they were. The end result was I lost about 40% of the sales force and several managers, yet the interesting thing was production actually went up after they left.

The six months I spent rebuilding the agency paid off for every-one. Everyone was earning more money, attitudes were better and I actually spent less money on marketing because the good sales people I had hired appreciated the gift of a referral. I wanted more for my co-workers, my family and, yes, for myself.

Volunteerism And You

Leadership opportunities within service organizations can be a wonderful training ground for the person who wants to develop the skills required to get people with various skill levels to voluntarily complete a project together. I admit I have a soft spot for veteran causes and artistic organizations, and where my actions are concerned, I can become myopic when volunteering for these types of causes.

Remember, when you work with various groups be careful that you do not become a volunteer junky. Volunteerism is great as long as it does not take away from your ability to lead yourself to economic success.

A very wise mentor coached me to understand responsible volunteerism. He recommended that a person stay in a leadership position for a maximum of two years with any one group. He went on to say that by subscribing to this approach, you show others that the organization is bigger than your personal need for recognition. You foster fresh ideas when you involve the participation of new people. Your main objective is to help develop a competent, enthusiastic replacement for your position. The whole idea is to give back and, hopefully, you have encouraged others to step into your position.

Be Yourself In Spite Of Yourself

Do not be a Jeckle and Hyde. How many times have you seen the boss/person-in-charge behave one way outside of the work environment and then assume a different identity while at work? What I am saying is do not take on a different persona while in charge because people will not want to work with you in future endeavors even if a paycheck is involved.

Behaving in a draconian manner will only alienate people. You will have high staff turn- over and incur all the related expenses of finding and training a replacement staff. Instead of focusing your energy on growing your business, you will continuously attempt to maintain your core goals and will never have the opportunity to expand your operation. You will never be able to develop people's skills and utilize their talents in your future business ventures.

Many people who work with me feel they are an important part of the success of the business for the simple reason that their opinion is always heard and, if it makes sense, their idea is implemented in the action steps. By allowing people to feel they have an "ownership" in the project enhances the chances of it being successfully completed.

Do Not Be A Patsy

Being supportive, inclusive, or being a good guy does not mean you should let your team or staff walk all over you. If a situation arises wherein a person does not participate responsibly with you and others in the company, you need to deal with it.

There was a sales manager working at my mortgage company who had a salary, bonuses and personal production incentives, and he decided he needed more even though he was not producing at any level. Another manager and he enjoyed inviting me out to lunch and a majority of the time I picked up the tab. I noticed they were not doing their job and were becoming evasive and combative when I questioned them about production at the weekly management meetings.

One day I invited them out to lunch and they eagerly accepted. As I was leaving the office, I mentioned that I needed to stop by Costco for something and invited them in while I grabbed some things. They were fine with that.

One of the things I love about Costco is that on certain days the food samples are fantastic. As we walked around, I encouraged them to sample the food and to, in fact, take two of each. After several samples, one of them stated that he needed to save room for lunch. That is when I informed them that this was their lunch because the free ride with me was over and they needed to produce business in 30 days.

One of them straightened up, the other became more defiant, so I let him go sooner than later because he had become disruptive in the work environment. Human Resources scolded me for the way I broached the issue at lunch. Thankfully, the facts were well documented so my decision was justified.

Gentle Humor Is Essential To Good Leadership

No matter how easy or difficult the project, do not be surprised if something goes wrong. How you respond will set the tone of how everyone else responds. You are the one who needs to have broad shoulders, so accept the situation and ask the person who made the mistake, "How are we going to fix it?" What is important is that they know you support them.

Listen To Your Partner

If you have a spouse or partner, talk to them and do not keep them in the dark, especially when things are not progressing the way you had planned. When you talk to your special person, make sure you have both ears open and the mouth shut when they talk.

The pearls of wisdom given to me by my wife have always enabled me to put things into perspective. If your partner is not supportive or you feel he or she does not understand the problem, do your partner and yourself a favor and seek professional help so both of your communication skills improve. Invest in your relationship, not in a triste. After 24 years of marriage, I feel my partner and I have done well together.

Knowledge Is Dangerous

Take the opportunity to avail yourself of some form of education to improve your skills. This will enable you to have the tools to keep your ideas fresh ideas and ensure your success, and do not forget to give yourself time to review your successes and things you think you need to improve on. Most of all, keep a gentle sense of humor.

"The manager asks how and when; the leader asks what and why."

Warren Bennis

Section 4:

Business Insights for Leadership

Lisa Wells

Lisa Wells founded Coast2Coast Business Support Solutions after more than 15 years in the real estate and information technology industries. As a Certified eMarketing Associate, Lisa specializes in helping coaches, consultants, entrepreneurs, and other independent and solo professionals manage their many online marketing needs.

Lisa has a Bachelor of Science degree in Business Management and is an active member of the International Virtual Assistants Association.

She lives in Jacksonville, North Carolina with her husband Richard, sons Eddie and Brett, and her dog Soochow.

Visit her on the web at www.Coast2CoastBusiness.com or read her many articles published on her blog at www.MarketingMindsetBlog.com.

You can also e-mail her at Lisa@Coast2CoastBusiness.com.

Chapter Sixteen

Find a Need and Fill It

Lisa Wells

A s soon as I stumbled upon the virtual assistance industry, I could see it was something unique. While so-called gurus are chanting "you must dominate the market" and selling secrets to "beat the competition," this is not the prevailing sentiment among virtual assistants. They all seem to have the same quiet confidence that there is more than enough work and clients to go around.

I'd like to tell you how I got started in this industry and became an entrepreneur. Whether you're still hanging on to that day job, or you're already at home and looking for a way to stay there, I hope you'll use the lessons I share as you're discovering your leader within.

Virtual Assistants- the Accidental Pioneers

I'm still not sure if I found the virtual work world or if it found me. Other virtual assistants have told me the same thing. The early pioneers, just 13 short years ago, were leading a huge new trend and they didn't even know it.

The International Virtual Assistants Association (IVAA) defines a virtual assistant as "an independent entrepreneur providing administrative, creative and/or technical services. Utilizing advanced technological modes of communication and data delivery, a professional VA assists clients in his/her area of expertise from his/her own office on a contractual basis."

Most virtual assistant businesses are born in the home office, out of a computer, knowledge of a particular market, and a burning desire to help that market while working from home. People are sometimes surprised to hear that I really enjoyed my career as an information technology specialist, and my children were very happy going to their daycare center for stories, arts and crafts and playtime. I had no intention of leaving my job to work at home.

From Southern California to North Carolina

No, instead something happened to us that happens to most military families; we got orders to move. We were living in Southern California, where I had lived my entire life, when my husband got orders to North Carolina.

My research quickly revealed that even though I had a bachelor's degree in business and 20 years of experience, there simply were no well-paying jobs. Sadly, this is the plight of many military spouses. I checked into telecommuting, transcribing, freelance web design and other work-at-home options, but nothing seemed to fit.

That summer, the movie "Robots" came out; a cute family movie about Rodney Copperbottom, an idealistic robot inventor. To foil the plans of an evil inventor, Rodney applies the philosophy of "find a need and fill a need," and succeeds in bringing his robot friends together to save Robot City.

Find a Need, Fill a Need

More than being one of the basic principles of business, this phrase goes right to the heart of what a virtual assistant does and how I came to be one. It also goes right to the heart of how you can evolve as a person and become a great leader in your world.

Before my career as an information technology specialist, I was a secretary and a word processor. While most of my colleagues lived and breathed computers, my passion and expertise for paperwork, data entry, and report formatting brought in excellent money and rewards. Rather than doing what everyone else did, I carved out a specialty and filled that need.

Humble Beginnings

I imagine that most virtual assistants start out like I did, by researching and asking lots of questions. I even sent emails to other virtual assistants asking if they had any openings, obviously not understanding that they were small business owners themselves.

I finally understood that if I wanted to succeed, I needed to get out there on my own, find my own clients, get my own website, and be my own boss. I needed to take the lead to develop my own business. Now I get those same types of emails and I reply as best as I can, pointing these new entrepreneurs in the right direction.

Starting a virtual assistant business is not a get-rich-quick scheme. After my first six months of working 12-hour days and nearly every weekend, I had made exactly $200. I had no clients, no niche, and no direction.

I was signing up for one business-building program after another, each promising me more clients, more money - you know the deal. I have seen many virtual assistants (and other entrepreneurs) fall into this trap.

Eventually, after another six months or so, I did get my act together. And within two years, I was completely replacing the income that I had been making at my previous job. How did I turn it around? By taking an honest look at my obstacles and moving past them.

My biggest obstacles were lack of self-confidence, not having a niche, and getting mired in the day to day tasks and losing focus of my goals and objectives. Honesty with oneself in a situation is a core strength of leaders. They inherently make decisions for themselves and their decisions have a direct impact on others too.

Lack of Self Confidence

I wish I could say that everyone who starts on the road to being a leader in their own life or even as a business owner will be successful, but unfortunately, many won't. Why not? They lack self-confidence and they're afraid to put themselves "out there."

Sadly, not only does this cheat them out of a fulfilling opportunity, it also cheats others in their future out of gaining from their knowledge, wisdom and unique message.

You may think, "Why would anyone want to hear what I have to say?" Frankly, there are people out there who can only hear your message from YOU. Maybe they've heard the same message before but it didn't resonate until they heard it from you, in your context, or in your authentic voice.

You do not need to be a millionaire or member of MENSA to have a positive impact on someone else's life or business - *and that's the key*. My clients benefit not only from my knowledge and skills, they're also tapping into the cumulative experiences of all of my previous clients.

What's Your Specialty?

You may think, "There are already so many other leaders out there. How will I stand out?" Write down all of the unique experiences that you've had in your personal and professional life. You might be surprised at your potential areas of expertise.

Some of my coaching clients are specializing in such diverse areas as business/career, communication, ADD/ADHD, abundance, getting clients, Christian living, the law of attraction, baby boomer entrepreneurs, productivity, and becoming a fearless female.

Each had their own unique experience to share and built their business upon it, standing out from the crowd at the same time. They are becoming leaders in their own area of experience.

You may have a hard time thinking of yourself as an expert, at first. I know I did. I felt like a fraud. It took a long time for me to overcome this obstacle and acknowledge my expert status, but I worked at it and I did it. Now I can say with confidence that I am an expert and that I provide expert services to my clients.

What about you? Do you have extensive knowledge about a particular subject? Well, then, you too are an expert. You have a foundation with that knowledge to lead others.

Try thinking about it this way: We are surrounded by medical experts, legal experts, and military experts and we don't hesitate to turn to them for their knowledge and expertise. Do they always agree or know everything about everything? No. But that doesn't mean they are not experts and they are certainly not frauds. Many are revered as leaders in their fields.

I want to make a case for choosing a specialty, or "niche," in your area of leadership. Many of my peers defend the "generalist" strategy because:
1) it's hard to say no to people when first starting out
2) they don't have a particular preference for one particular area or one set of tasks over another, and
3) they don't know what a target market is or how to reach one.

I started out as a generalist, advertising every possible service and task that I could perform, from desktop publishing to database design, from website design to word processing. Because I had previous experience and contacts in the real estate industry, I attracted real estate professionals as clients and claimed them as my niche.

Eventually, I realized that this wasn't the type of work I enjoyed doing. My clients called me at odd hours and work often stretched into the weekend. I didn't complain – I didn't have any other clients – but I wasn't happy.

Luckily, I had a business coach to talk it over with and finally decided that I was in the wrong niche. At the same time, I recognized that I felt a much stronger connection with the coaches and consultant clients that I was working with.

That weekend I changed my website, changed my newsletter, and declared my niche of coaches and consultants. Guess who I started getting inquires from? I believe this is what they refer to as the law of attraction and I saw first-hand how it worked in my business. By taking the risk of changing where I put my energies and focus I became a leader for a group of clients that I am best suited for.

Mired in the Minutiae

I was beginning to see the signs of success but my vision wasn't focused enough. Sure, I knew that I wanted more clients, but how many? If the law of attraction brings us exactly what we ask for, then all I could expect from that wish was one more client than I already had!

So I stopped sweating the small stuff and starting started looking at the bigger picture of my goals, objectives, and vision. For example, one of my objectives was to keep the weekends work-free and incorporate more play time. But my day-to-day actions were out of alignment with this. I was accepting clients who could only work in the evenings and weekends and wanted immediate turn-around. I had to make a conscious decision to stop this. I had to let my "big picture" philosophy drive my marketing efforts to attract the types of clients I wanted.

The best leaders are the ones who go out of their comfort zone and make a decision that not only benefits them but those around them. My choice to accept clients that fit with my vision and needs allowed me to grow and serve my clients better.

You Can Do This

You don't have to "beat the other guy" to be a great leader, but you do have to stop the negative self-talk, acknowledge that you're an expert, and hone in on your niche. Then, keep your focus on the big picture of what you want out of your desire to become a leader and how it will fit into your lifestyle, your passion, your values, and your schedule.

As quoted from Zig Ziglar, *"You can get everything in life you want, if you help enough other people get what they want."* So find that need and fill it!

Tracey Walker

Tracey Walker is an Expert Internet Network Marketer from Chicago, IL. She is also the co-founder of Home Solutions Group, Inc. a premier real estate investment company in Chicago. Currently, Tracey works with struggling networkers and helps them to see the sprawling down-lines they desire and at least a 4 figure monthly income from their business.

Tracey prides herself in providing the coaching and support that so many network marketers reach out for. She specifically shows her students HOW to market and locate people who are looking for them by using the internet. She has seen the traditional marketing methods of network marketing wipe out determined hardworking entrepreneurs and is dedicated to exposing that type of person to the true secrets of Network Marketing success.

She holds an MBA concentrated in marketing and is an active member of Delta Sigma Theta Sorority, Inc.

Email: tracey@traceywalkeronline.com
Web: www.TraceyWalkerOnline.com
Phone: 866-759-0579

Chapter Seventeen

Success in Leadership Through Systems

Tracey Walker

- No boss
- 10,000 sq ft home
- Buy whatever I want
- Go on vacation whenever I want
- Never have to worry about money or bills again

These are some of the reasons that I joined the Network Marketing Industry. I had done my research and I knew that the industry legitimately provided a way for an average person to start a business, with minimum investment and risk, and mold it into a multi-million dollar enterprise... if so desired. But when I joined, there seemed to be a plague on network marketing!

I mean everyone I talked to about it thought that it was a scam or some sort of get rich quick scheme. I found myself begging and even dishing out cash to entice my friends and family members to come to the meetings. I worked so hard with trying to coordinate the schedule of my up-line leader with that of my prospect so that "someone who really knew the business" could explain it to my potential team member. And then something happened.

I got trampled on, rejected and tossed out on the street with no new sign-ups. So I began to ask myself, *"How is it that I could see the opportunity to have a strong business and take the lead in developing something solid for my life- but nobody else could see the vision for themselves?"*

The company gave me a welcome kit and told me to set up my first home meeting and invite all my friends and family. I was instructed to buy the marketing materials provided by the company and share them with anyone who came within three feet of me.

I did what I was taught. I did what the top people in the company were doing – but it never developed into business for me. Heck, after all of that, I eventually resorted to the mindset of maybe this just wasn't for me.

Now the sad part about this is that somewhere in the process I lost sight of my dreams of working from home, spending more time with my family and buying anything I wanted anytime. I slowly began to join the long list of naysayers who "told me" that network marketing doesn't work for normal people.

I saw the people making 6 figures a year and thought that I could do it the way they did it, no problem. Ah ha! I took all the actions that made them successful, but that was the problem, and still is the problem with traditional network marketing.

Why didn't it work for me? I began to understand that it was not my fault. To begin, it didn't work because I did not have a proven, measurable system to follow nor was I set up with the right tools or strategy _for me_.

Deep down inside I knew that this type of business model can certainly be done. I mean, if it were impossible, all of those people on the stage at the conventions wouldn't even be there. So, what is it that was missing? What was it that the heavy-hitters knew and had that I didn't? Well the answer was so simple that I didn't even get it the first time I heard it. "A system!"

That was it! The Multi-million dollar earners had a duplicable system that worked based on metrics, not on chance. It was the system all along that they looked to as a model for leadership to guide their actions and approach to the business.

Now I could see why I simply could not succeed using the system my personal up-line leaders taught me. THEY were succeeding, but I was not. It was because I was trying to plug into a system where only the strong personalities could survive, where the extroverts got all the leads and the one who could present was adored. My personality is different. As my leaders, they didn't see that I wasn't just like them. I needed a leader who understood my style. Great leaders identify quickly that all people cannot be led the same way and then the leaders adapt their teaching style to achieve results for all.

Motivated by my revelation about the system I had been taught, I turned to a person whom I knew could provide me with quality leadership and honest answers in this area. My new mentor showed me that being successful in this business model didn't require me to go through the well worn system of calling from the phone book and/or put every person I came in contact with on my "top 100 prospect list".

It didn't require that I be the best speaker or even the savvy salesman (even though I think I'm pretty good at that). Being successful in this business model only required *me to be me* and to *use the skills and talents that I already knew I possessed in a way that would compel others,* on their own, to want to be part of whatever it was I had. I had finally got it! I needed to develop my own system of leadership that would work for me!

So How Did I Turn Failure Into Success?

Taking the lead to build my business, the first thing I did was get started developing a successful system that would support my style of leadership and communication. I learned how to market so people would want to search out my services and then I developed a system for it. That is exactly what I teach my students.

Most network marketers still don't get it. Most business owners do not get it. The world is not your market. Everybody doesn't want what you have. I had to stop being the hunter and become the hunted. Once I began being sought out, my business began to grow.

The second thing I did was determine who I was as a leader, what skills and qualities I had and I began to use them. Many people

I have coached said once they sat down and allowed themselves to emerge, so did the wealth that was hidden in their business.

For example, I loved to speak in front of audiences, so I put systems in place to help me capitalize on that. The internet is full of services that allow my potential prospects to hear me. I had to let the true leader within me come out and not be afraid of the success that would follow!

The third step I took was to equip myself with the right tools for success. See, if you try to build a house without nails and a hammer, you're going to struggle unnecessarily. Likewise, if you try to build a successful business without a specific set of tools, you will wind up broke and part of the NFL (No Friends Left) club. Before understanding the importance of leadership through strong systems that would support my style I had already become a hall-of-famer of the NFL!

Now, normally I save what I'm going to share with you for my special coaching students, but this book is special and so are you. I dug deep and unfailingly until I found someone to share with me the specific tools I would need to win in this business. This mentor put me on a right path to get set up with technology tools that would integrate into the person to person side of my business system. I chose to listen to what the ultra-successful people were telling me and the results started pouring in.

The final thing I did was align myself with a mastermind group, one that was dedicated to the growth and development of its members.

Remember those naysayers we talked about earlier? I decided to let them be them and move to a place of positivity and optimism. Get involved with a group where the energy and the teachings produce success stories and wealth. This one step has allowed me to really take control of my life and design a brand new blueprint for the next 3-5 years.

My Leaders Didn't Know About This Stuff, I Didn't Have Any Support

What I want to make crystal clear to you is that it doesn't matter what company, what product, or who your current manager or up-line is. Leadership and support is always available to those who seek it out. I didn't like the results, or lack thereof, that I was initially getting from my so called leaders, so I sought out the information on my own.

I sought to align myself with those leaders who would see in me what I couldn't initially see for myself. My new leaders allowed me to learn, grow and encouraged me to develop in a way that will support me for years.

I firmly believed that I had to make this happen for me. I had to take matters into my own hands. To become a great leader in my own right, I had to believe that I could succeed and then I needed to find alternate solutions to teach me how to really make it happen.

By becoming my own leader first, I was able to teach my team exactly what I had learned and discovered. Being willing to share the knowledge rather than be afraid of creating competition for myself is a trait of a confident leader. That action resulted in a solid organization full of strong, secure, confident professional business leaders in their own right. All I simply needed to do was make a shift from a system that did not work to one that did. And believe it or not, this revolutionary system of leadership worked!

In many business models there is a high failure rate. Many of the network marketing industry's high-dollar earners make excuses like "high attrition is expected" or "you have to get a lot of no's before you get your yes" just to keep new reps pushing. Hogwash! Yes attrition is high, but for a very different reason. Attrition in network marketing and failure in most businesses are due to a lack of planning and a strong system that supports the vision of the company.

The system needs to support the different personality types that will be following and implementing it. The system also needs leaders that can teach, inspire and recognize when the system needs modification for the people following it. Business evolves. Systems need to evolve too if they do not work anymore.

I understand now that if I come across someone who is not looking for a change, by their own admission, then even if temporarily convinced, he/she will eventually return back to what is most comfortable.

Moral of the story: I have mastered how to find and work with people who raise their hands and decide that they too want to work with me. They too want to become leaders in their own right.

Top 5 Questions To Ask Yourself When The Going Gets Tough

1. Is leadership success (or whatever it is you want) something you deeply want and are willing to work hard at or is it just a thought that passes by every now and then?

2. Why do you have to make "this" work? Who and what is counting on you?

3. What skill(s) do you have that you can capitalize on and use to differentiate yourself from the crowd?

4. Are you coachable and teachable as well as open to critiquing that will only make you better?

5. Are you excited about the life that you know you can have and ready to go for it?

Before I experienced my network marketing success, I asked myself these very same questions. And you know what? I was honest with myself too! The answers revealed to me that I was ready to let the leader within me come out and that I was serious about making a difference in me and my family's lifestyle.

So, take a moment and ask yourself these exact same questions. You might even need to take a day or so to come up with the true answers.

Although I don't know what your final answers will be, I do know that if they are anything like mine you will do and be just what you said you could do and be- a phenomenon!

Allow yourself to fail and grow in search for your leadership success, knowing that it's part of the learning process. Just don't stop searching... success is on the way... even for YOU!

Ryan Hill

Ryan Hill is an online marketing expert and owes his knowledge to his determination and manifestation to be successful.

He has many specialties/knowledge including html, web design, blogging, rss feeds, adwords, adsense, safe-lists, forums, groups, free advertising, solo-ads, social networking, video networking, and so much more that takes years off the learning curve of his marketing students.

Ryan is 27 years old, married with one child and lives in beautiful Fayetteville, TN.

Contact Info for Ryan Hill:
Web: www.RyanHillonline.com
Email: RyanHill.PCN@gmail.com
Instant Messengers:
Skype ID: Ryan.Hill.Mentor
ooVoo ID: RyanHill
Phone: (931)625-0624

Chapter Eighteen

Indentify Your Leadership Skills

Ryan Hill

What skills do you think make a great leader? For myself I be-lieve the following are essential to being a great leader in today's business arena:

Mindset

Having knowledge and skill sets in your field is important for success as a leader. Your knowledge and experience are impor-tant to support fulfillment of your product or service. However, having knowledge isn't always enough. To be a great leader and reach new levels in your business, you must continue to invest your time into mindset training.

Your mindset and inner self consists of how you speak, where your thoughts roam, your successful or negative thinking, and this list goes on. Your mind controls every action you take in your life. This area of your inner self has the potential to always be improving, even if you are already 'successful' in your busi-ness.

The most successful business owners focus on improving their inner self and learning how to discipline their mindset to attract success. (Often the people who are the most successful do this the most diligently.)

A good exercise to bring this practice into your daily habits is to sit upright in a chair, close your eyes, and sit there for 15 to 30 minutes. Be as still as you possibly can and just inhale and breathe. Through this, each time you exhale, let your stress and everything go out with the breath. Feels good doesn't it? Doing this everyday will help you to learn how to control your thoughts and release negative energy.

Leadership involves stepping into areas that others may not be comfortable with. If you are going to be a leader, controlling your thinking is important to instill the confidence others will have in you. Mental preparation will help you through those times where you may not have much practical experience. Your mentor can educate and guide you with knowledge and their experiences. Visualization of yourself in that same situation will make you ready for any situation.

The brain does not differentiate between reality and imagined thought. Little by little, you will be imprinting successes in your brain. As you walk forth, when you have opportunity to apply these areas of growth, you will have a foundation on which to build new success! Once you are not afraid to receive it, you may achieve it. You need to visualize it first and believe that you already have it.

Some people find it beneficial to work with a mentor or coach during success training exercises. Your coach or mentor will help you with an action plan and should start you off at whatever knowledge level you are currently. After you continue to learn and develop your knowledge, that leadership role will be passed down to you when you're ready. Don't force this issue. It does take time, and varies on how much time you put into your business.

Enter the Sales Person

If you think you're not a sales person, think again. Each of us has inherent skills that allow us to 'sell' ourselves every day. We may not see ourselves as that but once you understand that selling as a leader is not about hard pressuring people into a decision- then it's easier to see how this mindset plays into your ability to be becoming successful.

One thing to understand about the way people like to be sold today is it's not about hard selling your product or service. Let's go over that again, it's not about hard selling your product or service! You may ask *"Ryan, how will I make money if I don't try to sell my products?"* It's very simple. Wherever you choose to land your career just make sure you are passionate for the company and what they stand for. After that it's about building a connection between you and your prospect. It's about building trust and credibility. Only then, after a person truly likes you as an individual, will they buy your product or service from you.

So it's not about being a high pressure sales person, it's about being a real person towards your customer or client. This is one of the main keys to success. Friends buy stuff from each other, and that's what you want them to do right? So let's quit treating them like a 'dollar' and start treating them like a friend.

As a leader, sometimes you need to sell ideas to those you are in charge of. This same principle applies. By building trust and a connection with the people you are in charge of, you will be more effective when you lead. Your passion and your commitment to a bigger unified vision with those around you will help sell your ideas for you.

Sales are important in any endeavor. Without sales, things become stagnant. Kids 'sell' to their parents. Parents 'sell' ideas to their children. As a leader you will have to 'sell' ideas, vision and commitment to your charges, and of course, in business sales produce the bottom line.

If you are not comfortable selling, this is an area that your mentor or coach can support you. Just ask! There are many valuable, easy to understand resources to help you grow in this area. Remember though; when you learn sales technique stay true to yourself. Keep your personality in your conversation- and you will do well.

Building Relationships

Building relationships with professional people can very quickly turn into friendships. This action of communicating with others will help support your business growth – and will help you develop a key skill in leadership: active listening.

When you start a conversation with someone online or offline, you are getting to know this person. At this stage you are not trying to sell him or her anything. You are just getting to know them as a human being. You want to find out where they live, if they are married, how many kids they have, what they do for a living and what hobbies they enjoy. Let the conversation sway where it will. You're trying to build a relationship in which you've taken the time to genuinely be interested in and you listened to the answers. People don't care about how much you know… until they know how much you care.

I built a friendship online over 5 years ago and we live about 9 hours away from each other. Would you have imagined that I still speak to him on a daily basis and we visit each other yearly? This is how powerful friendships become.

This is not just a technique to make more money. It is the way of life in any successful business. It's also an element to identify in yourself. Can you engage in genuine conversation with others and patiently, attentively listen? If so, you have the makings of a great leader. If you're not quite there yet, this is a great skill to develop. It will serve you well everywhere.

When people see that you possess the skill to really, and I mean really listen to them- you can lead them. Trust is built quickly because you care enough to connect with them.

The very successful business people you see around you in your day to day travel, all use this very simple secret in their business. Have you ever spoken to a person and even if you are in a room full of others, they give you their sole attention? How did that make you feel? The best leaders learn to connect with everyone on a genuine level.

In addition to listening, you can succeed in business and as a leader by asking the right questions. Ask people questions about themselves. Then listen. Listen and you will lead.

Branding Yourself

Branding yourself is critical to your success as a leader online or offline. Branding yourself means exactly the way it sounds. You must become your own individual and show people the real you. Don't act like someone you're not, just be yourself. Speak to someone like they are already your friend. Personal branding involves letting people get to know you through your first and last name, not just your business name.

There are many styles of leaders and many tactics to practical leadership. When you are consistent with your style, you will brand yourself. It's not always about promotion or marketing of your business. It's about consistency in representing who you are and the communication you have with those you lead. People will hear your business name and they think of you personally if you branded yourself as one who is dependable, listens, is willing to learn, and really cares about others.

Succeed By Finding a Coach/Mentor That Can Help You!

To succeed at anything, regardless of the topic, top leaders speak of the importance of learning from someone who has already been successful in that particular area. If you want to succeed with a business, find a person that has been successful in that business before and engage them as your mentor or coach.

Conclusion

People that are looking to become more successful in business or have found their leader within ultimately will find benefit in mentoring or coaching with someone they can relate to.

You can't always relate to everyone but there's great opportunity to learn and grow in the discovery of your mentors. I can't stress enough about really finding a coach that is supportive of your success. Be passionate about the company you work for. Be passionate about the endeavors you wish to step up and lead. Communicate regularly with honesty to your mentors and coaches. Tell them you want to see what they teach and train.

When you feel comfortable that he/she is the right mentor/coach for you- be ready to ask them questions and be willing to actively listen to them as well. Let them lead you to success so you can eventually turn around and be the mentor or coach to lead others to success as well.

I want to leave you with this, I wish you the best of success in anything that you do and may God bless your life and family.

"The final test of a leader is that he leaves behind him in other men the conviction and the will to carry on."

Walter Lippman

David L. Feinstein

David L. Feinstein, noted business coach and home business entrepreneur, is the author of various articles that help to empower individuals to excellence. He has become a success coach and mentor to many thousands of people who are looking for a better lifestyle and desire to achieve success.

David and Ann are 20 plus year home-based-business entrepreneurs and have built their international business into over 25 countries. During the past 20 years they have become two of the most notable experts in the network marketing industry and today their network has more than 47,000 members!

Recently they've created the Agel Diamond System found at www.buildingdynamicfutures.com which is a totally 100% duplicable system to get members of their organization from zero to Agel Diamond level in record speed, using all of the tactics and techniques that have proven totally effective over the last 20 years. They've combined that with the latest Internet Marketing techniques and technology that leaves their organization light-years ahead of their competition.

Web: www.annanddavidfeinstein.com
Email: davidf@pbiworld.com
Phone: 215-321-1400

Chapter Nineteen

How to Create the Leaders that Will Propel Your Business!

David & Ann Feinstein

Whenever the question of leadership comes up regarding my business I often have to reflect on what leadership traits have gotten Ann and I, my wife and partner, where we're at in the last 20 years.

No matter what type of business or organization you belong to, I believe that there are all types, shapes, and sizes of leaders in this world, and one type may not be as fitting in one area or industry as in another.

Certainly the types of leaders that the armed services create are important and obviously have helped shaped an entire nation... yet some of those traits and techniques that these leaders possess may not be quite as effective in some working environments. They may seem quite overbearing for instance for an elementary school teacher, of whom obviously must also possess strong leadership skills for shaping our children's minds. The truth is that there is no one size fits all type of leader.

How does one decipher between the skills that have led to dramatic success? Rewinding back through the 20 plus years of success that Ann and I have in the network marketing industry, and our very fast success that we've achieved in our latest business venture with Agel Enterprises – there are a variety of traits I feel have led us to where we are. However, I believe that above all, the most crucial trait that we both possess, and that nearly every other leader in business, possesses as well, is quite simple.

Caring For Those You Lead

The number one leadership quality that we identified is that we profoundly care for every single person in our organization. In fact, we enjoy seeing them succeed and achieve their dreams perhaps as much, if not more, as we do for ourselves. (Actually, we get downright excited about it.) This is essential to have success as a leader, bottom line!

Genuinely caring about PEOPLE is a leadership skill that is easy to find inside yourself. If you are the type of person that naturally is drawn to empowering or the betterment of others, you've just identified a seed for your leadership opportunity.

Whether your organization is large and wide, or small and intimate, being able to get people to follow you... to follow your lead... quite frankly takes more than simply caring about their success. The fact is, however, that without that one paramount asset, as a leader, you will not get very far. That leadership quality is the one that sets the foundation for all others.

Creating Growth

The other vital element to having success in business and as a leader of others is the reality that when you lead, and create successes within an organization, you do so by not just doing alone, nor by simply pointing the way and delegating tasks. In fact, doing those things does not really make leaders at all but rather an organization dependent on the leader.

Absolutely no business organization in the world or nation can survive without independent free thinking leaders throughout. These free thinkers need to be taught to communicate and support one another to achieve a larger vision. This is why Ann and I, along with many leaders throughout history, dedicate time and energy to actually creating leaders.

Know the traits it takes to become powerful magnetic leaders and mentors, you, finding your leadership style, will want to help shape those who come into your organization with leadership traits. Very carefully and attentively mold each one who shows a desire to perform the actions that will also lead men and women to success.

Try to instill in these people the importance of caring for their own organization. Leadership starts at the top and travels all the way down to the person who just became a team member yesterday. Again, this is one of the key reasons that we've been as successful as we have been. Every single person on the team deserves the opportunity to step up and learn. As a leader it is a huge disservice not emphasizing that fact and creating the opportunity for others to grow.

Now of course there are other characteristics of a genuine leader. For those who have trust in you and decided to follow your lead, understand that not every person is born with the attributes of a natural outgoing leader. In fact most people are not initially comfortable as leaders. They may not have all the skill sets it takes right out of the gate to influence and inspire others to follow them. This means that you, after you've found your leadership style must shape and mold them. It is essential to focus on this for future success of your business or organization.

We have also come to understand that it is important to place goals and ambitions likely much greater than that of those which we lead. As a leader in business, for our team, it allows us to see the big picture. These goals allow us to actually see what's possible for all the members of our team in order to motivate them to keep persisting through the hard times. If you are the top leader already or are leading others while working with a mentor, keeping your vision bigger than that of those you are in charge of allows them to reach a higher potential.

Persistent Leadership

Persistence is another absolute must when it comes to leading people who are willing to follow you. Obstacles will be met. The persistence to either push through and clobber these obstacles, or take the time and thought to work your way around them takes a ton of perseverance. Although it's important that people have this trait innately, it's also important to know that this can be taught. Using such elements as optimism, critical thinking, and visionary skills, most any person can be taught to think and act persistently and work through until the ultimate goal is achieved.

It is important to recognize however that persistence and determination should not be confused with stubbornness and resistance to change. In fact, we make it a point to remind ourselves and our team that while it's not necessary to reinvent the wheel... and that it is recommended to make great use of other people's trial and error for a shortcut to success... we should also recognize and benefit from the fact that with new technology comes new opportunity. Trying to ignore and avoid this fact is detrimental to your business.

Stay constantly ahead of the loop by having frequent contact and consultation with outside leading experts in order to stay way ahead of the technology curve. You do not have to know everything yourself. Just know who to go to so that you, as a leader, can continue to learn as well. This keeps us, our system, and our organization on the cutting edge of the very latest modern technology and leaves us leaps ahead of nearly all of our competition.

You can do the same with your leadership roles. Instead of resisting change, realize that embracing it is a key factor in propelling success. Not being flexible while technology advances breeds struggles for others for years with the same old tired methods.

It's important to note that through all we do and teach as leaders, it is important to be very careful to always do everything that we do with integrity along with the perspective of doing things right and ethical.

One thing we've learned and witnessed a number of times is that no matter how much it may seem as though doing things unethically can lead to a shortcut to success –KNOW that the truth is: quick successes often lead to quicker failures. Great leaders conduct business and all interactions with others with the mindset that what is being created is a lifelong and lasting opportunity.

Leading the way with ethics, a system to teach others and a vision that combines efforts of a whole team, work together toward one common goal. For us it is to live with more freedom and joy than we ever thought possible. What is your goal? What is your vision? Lead by example.

On any given day you can find us doing exactly what we teach our future leaders in our organization to do: Grow their own businesses consistently and systematically. Our Agel organization means the world to us. Our wish is that each and every person we teach and lead sees success and also becomes a great leader in their own right.

May you also see great success as a leader in your industry and area of life!

"Whoever is providing leadership needs to be as fresh and thoughtful and reflective as possible to make the very best fight."

Faye Wattleton

Section 5:

Extra Insights to Great Leadership

Ben Gay III

Ben Gay III is a world famous Sales Trainer/Author/Consultant, the person who brought us "The Closers" series (called "the core documents of modern selling") and the powerful Master Closers Sales Training Seminars. He's also authored 12 other books on the subjects of selling and living successfully while ghost writing another dozen or so for other sales trainers/speakers/seminar leaders/coaches/consultants.

Ben also writes a newsletter "The Closers Update" that's been called "the voice of professional selling". He created and taught the famous "People Builders" program for the inmates and staff at California's infamous San Quentin State Prison. He was nicknamed "The Attitude Coach" for the Apollo 15, 16 & 17 astronauts by Col. James Erwin, Commander of Apollo 15. Then, in 1976, Ben launched the "800 Number Industry" by founding "The National Communications Center", the very first "call center".

Ben Gay was also the founder and is the current Executive Director of the National Association of Professional Salespeople. And through his coaching, consulting, books, audio programs, video programs, newsletters, teletraining sessions, speeches, seminars and his countless TV & radio appearances, he has helped train, directly and indirectly, literally millions of other professional salespeople around the world!

For the very best in sales training systems and material, contact:

Ben Gay III

THE CLOSERS

(800) 248-3555

WWW.BFG3.COM

Chapter Twenty

The Yellow Door

Ben Gay III

Reminiscing on my rise into leadership positions, I fondly recall specific moments that shaped me into the person I am now. It is clear to me, in retrospect, that during our lifetimes, we have opportunities that can frame our thinking and help define who we are.

Among the marks of great leaders is the ability to identify those moments as they occur – and then, later, recall them. By simply allowing them to stay rooted in our thoughts, we remain aware of the things that made us successful along the way. Great leaders always remember where they came from. And they keep a vision of where they are going.

One of my first recollections as a young, up-and-coming entrepreneur was that I didn't know I could fail! I really didn't know that most people thought "you aren't supposed to succeed." But I was fortunate in that, in the neighborhood where I spent my childhood, I was surrounded by very successful businessmen (it was only businessmen back then!).

"Succeed" was simply what you did. Everywhere I looked, I saw success physically manifested in the form of lovely homes, nice lawns, luxury cars, and in the conversations of the men who spoke of their businesses.

And it probably didn't hurt that Atlanta's famous East Lake Country Club (Bobby Jones' home course) was a block and a half down the street – where my family had been members for years.

But it wasn't until much later that I realized I'd been exposed to a vision of what success really looked like! I'd been exposed to the great leaders in the Atlanta community and to many others who were "The Captains of Industry" in a much larger world. So understand, "the thought processes of success" had been defined clearly for me early on. Success was within reach! It was normal! People will support and help one another! I saw people leading and inspiring others all around me! I simply didn't know any better. Lucky me!

But there was another key moment. This one lesson led me to a path which helped make me one of the top professionals in the sales world – and a multimillionaire. I was 14, and at that point in my life, I just wanted to earn some money. So my father gave me his blessing (and his lawnmower!) and off I went to start my own lawn mowing business.

With my attention to detail, I did pretty well for myself. I offered great customer service, tidiness and timeliness. But then it happened! I reached a point where I personally couldn't take on any new clients. I was doing well, the referrals were coming in, but there were only so many hours in the day! Probably still are, I assume.

The results of my attention to detail, and always trying to do my best, were about to become another learning opportunity for me!

So I went to my father/mentor and we talked about it. Dad was a sharp businessman, long a leader in the community. Instead of teaching me to be "OK" with the status quo, he gave me new insights and information. He always taught through example. What he shared then was how to "leverage my time" by learning new skills. He showed me that these new skills, coupled with my personal efforts, could impact people's lives for a greater good. He taught me how to create a win-win-win situation!

He taught me "The Art & Science of Selling," along with the importance of delegation and management. A leader himself, he taught me how to be a leader within my own neighborhood. Here I was - age 14 - and I understood that, if I wanted to, I could grow my lawn mowing company. And that, if I wanted to reach a bigger goal, I had to enlist the efforts of others. I had to sell other kids on "the vision" of working for me.

I had to create a vision and build trust amongst my customers by backing up what I said. I had to follow through on my word. I also had to lead, inspire, teach, and learn how to manage my friends to make sure they did the job I was selling.

These skills laid a foundation that allowed me to achieve the success I have today - and it all started because my father saw my leadership potential. He reached out and taught me. He inspired me. He helped me to see "the leader" within myself. And he stood aside in order to let me find my own way in applying these skills.

A great leader knows when to inspire; a great leader knows when to delegate. The best leaders understand that, first, you must be the student. Amongst my peers at 14, I was a leader. We were literally the wealthiest 14 year olds around, and it all started out because I sought direction from someone who had shown me he knew how to be successful. I was willing to learn from a mentor. Today I am able to take the same basic principles I learned when I was 14 and teach them to millions of people around the world.

Another defining moment that shaped me into the person I am today was when I married.

Remember, I grew up in an environment where men were strong and they showed manifestations of their success by physical things. But then, after I moved out of my parents' home, I lived the life of a typical, young bachelor. I was "making it" on my own. My bachelor pad was simple - with 'guy furniture' and 'guy things'. "Simple," mainly.

I never really gave any of this a second thought until I moved "my things" out of my bachelor pad - and into "the home" in which my new bride and I were to reside.

After all of those days of living as a bachelor, "my things" never bothered me. But, now that I had a new bride to take care of, those same things simply wouldn't do. They were not good enough for her. I needed to create a home for us.

The desire to want more, and the unsettled feeling that comes from the status quo, is another characteristic within an up and coming leader. The motivation to 'do something' comes from an unsettled feeling with the way things are, or the way things have "always been." Most times, a leader is not motivated purely by a self-need. Often, the best leaders are motivated to improve, change, take care of, and teach/inspire others so that they may have something better!

To achieve this, you have to have a willingness to grow, a willingness to put yourself in a position of unfamiliar territory. Discovering "the leader within" awakens a desire that is stronger than self. It is about continuing the cycle of learning, growing, teaching and then giving back. Most people just need some direction to achieve great things - but it takes a person willing to give some direction to help put those opportunities into motion.

When you look at yourself and start to identify your leadership abilities, remember this:

Great leaders are always willing to improve. They also understand that, when they communicate with others, "the best of the best" will focus all of their attention on the person to whom they speak - blocking out all others to give undivided attention to the one to whom they speak. It's a "skill set" to practice and refine.

Once you've found your leadership potential, it's time to learn! I clearly remember one of the biggest defining moments in my whole career. This one event solidified for me the desire to really be the best I could be. In 1965 I was working for a man named Bill Patrick. I was later hired by his company to be one their sales trainers.

One day, I was with a group of other trainers teaching our students how to sell. We all had a training manual to teach from. I had accidentally left mine in an adjacent room and, when I went to retrieve it, I overheard a conversation that changed me forever!

I overheard Bill Patrick, the owner of the company, talking to the president; they were talking about me. Bill had apparently seen my leadership potential and had just watched a video of me at work. He made this statement: "I will pay more for the ability to communicate and lead than any other skills... and Ben has them!

Quickly and quietly, I left the room. And I left with a changed perspective and understanding of what others find truly valuable. From that moment on, I made a commitment to myself to take every opportunity to learn, grow and refine my skills as a communicator and leader.

I had seen my leadership potential early on, but now I was ready to truly embrace it. Before this moment, making money to provide for my family and live a life that I was accustomed to as a young boy was my motivation. But acknowledgment from others regarding my abilities became a much stronger motivator and opened the door to learning even more!

Part of my growth has always come from having interesting friends and putting myself into situations that have allowed me to speak with, study and learn from these colorful people. Leadership can be seen everywhere and in every circumstance. The best leaders always see learning opportunities.

When you find the leader within yourself, here are a couple of things to understand and always remember. First, leadership comes with privilege. You receive privilege as a leader, but the best leaders remember where they came from. They understand that, with that leadership, they are now responsible for those they lead.

If you use your leadership for the benefit of all, it's a win-win-win situation. You deserve to reap the rewards and accolades for a job well done! But if you choose to use your leadership skills to the detriment of others, you also deserve the negative consequences that come with it.

Last, as an up and coming leader finding your way, I share with you "The Yellow Door".

My good friend, the late great Ray Considine, who was a great leader in his own right, was at the launch of a major entertainment event with his family and some friends. Everyone there for the event was standing in line to get into the front door. As it was the grand opening of the attraction, the line and wait were long. Two or three hours!

Ray, being the consummate leader, decided not to have his friends and family wait that long. He looked around the location and, off to the back side of the building, he spotted a bright yellow door. It was the back door to the building. Not being one to settle for the status quo, he took action!

He went to the door and found a worker. Ray spoke to him as only Ray could. A few minutes later, Ray, his friends and his family, were inside the new exhibit – right up front! – only they had entered through "The Yellow Door"!

The wait time? About 5 minutes. But everyone else waited for hours! The moral of "The Yellow Door" story is this: Leaders always know there is another way. If you have found your leader within, and if you are ready to engage and grow, remember that, if your first approach at leadership doesn't turn out the way you wanted it, there's always another solution! If your results fall short - keep trying! Keep learning! Keep growing! "The Yellow Door" is everywhere - just seek the alternate solution and allow your leader within to thrive!

Over the past 40+ years, I've had the privilege of traveling all over the world and have been thrust into thousands of "interesting" experiences and opportunities – some big, some small. And, thanks to Ray Considine, I have almost always found "The Yellow Doors" of life.

"I cannot give you the formula for success, but I can give you the formula for failure, which is: Try to please everybody."

Herbert B. Swope

Kathy David

Kathy David is the CEO and President of IT TechPros, Inc. In this role, Kathy looks after all aspects of her business, including business development and business strategies. She is a qualified Business Professional and is an Alumni of UCLA – The Anderson School of Management, where she studied in Business Development and Entrepreneurship.

Kathy is no stranger to running a business. Prior to starting her I.T. Consulting business more than 2 years ago, Kathy spent 9 years in the banking industry working for a Fortune 500 Bank. The last 6 years of her career at the bank, she was an Assistant Vice President and Bank Manager which taught her the importance of successfully running a business and training successful sales teams.

After a successful career in banking, and starting her own company at an early age of 28, Kathy now inspires other people to act towards achieving their goals and dreams. Kathy's success and background in business, in professional and in personal development, has helped open doors of opportunities to help people realize their full potential.

E-mail: kdavid@it-techpros.com
Phone: 858-414-3056
Website: www.it-techpros.com

Chapter Twenty One

If You Think You Can, You Are Right!

Kathy David

I was just 19 years old and found myself waiting to be interviewed by the Market Area Manager of a Fortune 500 bank in San Diego, CA. I had applied for the Personal Banker position that was open for one of the branches in the area. I had no previous banking experience and no previous formal sales experience either. I was thinking to myself, "I really want this job and I know I don't have much experience, but there is no reason why I should not get this job!"

A few moments passed and I was called into the room. There she was, the Market Area Manager. She was very poised, professional, and she emitted a very strong and powerful energy that was very intimidating. I was invited to sit and I sat down in a chair in front of her. For a few moments we were both silent while she reviewed my resume. Then she looked up at me and asked, "Why are you applying for this position when you don't even have any sales or banking experience?" Now let's pause for a few minutes and let me tell you what I did prior to that moment.

I had been a waitress at a local restaurant and I worked about 30 hours a week in the evenings from four in the afternoon until midnight. In the mornings I took classes at the local community college. During this time I was very displeased with my current financial and living situation.

Deep inside I just knew I should be doing something greater than waiting on customers or tables. I knew I was more capable and could offer so much more to a business. I also knew I was not going to grow personally and professionally if I didn't do anything about my current situation. Realizing I would have to make a drastic change for me to change my situation, I decided to pursue a position that I thought at the time was out of my league.

Willing to take a chance and put myself out there, I took a risk and decided to make a big change in my life. Leaders often are not complacent with status quo and they are willing to reach above their boundaries. I was ready to do the same. Asking myself, "If I can have my ideal job, what would it be?" My answer was "A Banker." There was no research or due diligence done on my part with my decision to picking Banker as my ideal profession. I just thought that it would be a fun and interesting job for me to learn.

This decision led me to get the interview with the Market Area Manager of a bank, interviewing for a Banker position that even my resume or experience could not support or justify!

So now back to the interview. She asked me, "Why are you applying for this position when you don't even have any sales or banking experience?" I looked at her and said, "I know that I don't have the ideal experience you typically look for in a banker but I want to let you know that I am a very driven individual.

I am an action taker and I will do whatever it takes to learn and do any job or task that is given to me, regardless of how small or big it is. I would do myself and the company a disservice if I didn't make sure that the branch I will support and the company is not successful. I know that it is a big risk to go with someone that has no prior experience but I am also taking a risk in a applying for this position. I decided to apply anyway because I am taking a risk to become successful…" The interview lasted for about 40 minutes and I am very pleased to let you know that she offered me the job before I left her office.

I learned a valuable lesson that day that still supports decisions I make today. People are willing to give you a chance if you are willing to step up. Another thing I learned is the importance in conviction of your beliefs. Conviction and passion to follow through on a decision will carry you far. Others will see it and will support you when your vision is strong.

About a year and a half later I was promoted to Assistant Manager. Two years after that to Assistant Vice President of my own local branch managing up to 25 employees. During my time as a Bank Manager I received numerous awards and recognition of achievements for being top sales performer and top manager in my area during my career.

While I was closing and locking the branch one evening, I remembered thinking to myself: "Wow, if I can do this without having a college degree and just having a little bit of self determination, persistence, drive, and vision, what else can I accomplish if I put my mind and self to it?" At that moment I realized that I can have and do anything I wanted regardless- even if I was unclear on how it could happen.

Achieving goals and dreams starts with determination and the ability to look at oneself and see what skills you have today. What benefit can you bring forth with who you are now-and what can you learn to add to that ability? Leadership acknowledges where you are today and builds upon that. That was one of the turning points in my life. I realized that all things are possible and there is no limit to what can be achieved regardless of what circumstances may look like.

Accomplishing so much at a young age freed me from the bondage of typical stereotypes in the business world. People say that you need to have a college degree to make good money and be successful. They say you need to have a business degree to make it and be accepted in the business world. (Now I am not saying that education is not important. *Education is very important.* Getting education in your field is very important because without it, you cannot possibly achieve as much or be as successfully without increased knowledge.)

What I am saying is that getting what you want in life and wanting to be successful has little to do with a college diploma. *It has everything to do with your own determination and will for making success happen for you. The willingness to lead your destiny to an outcome that you create is one way success can manifest.*

Until I really came to the full understanding that your determination and your ability to invest in your self is a foot hold on greatness, I did stress out sometimes thinking I needed to finish college. I took night and online classes in hopes of completing my degree. Eventually I came to acknowledge that I would be fine without a degree. This change in my perspective allowed me to be guilt free with this decision.

Personally and professionally knowing that I am good enough and that I can continue to learn as I need to propelled me to really grow. No longer thinking that I needed to have a Bachelor's or a Master's Degree to accomplish the things I wanted for myself and my life, I created mental and emotional freedom to pursue whatever I wanted for myself.

I was 28 years old when I finally ended my career as a Banker. In 2006 I joined my husband and started our company, IT Tech-Pros, Inc. I am now the CEO of the company, and in charge of growing the business. In less than a month of starting our operations, we were already making money. Within a year, both my husband and I were supported by our business financially. Within a few months after that, we were able to hire a few full time staff members to help up with the growth and future success of our company.

IT TechPros, Inc. is an information technology company providing outsourced IT services to businesses in So. California. I am happy to share with you that I had no previous experience in the industry and was the worst when it came to computers!

All I knew about IT, before I became co-owner of our company, was email and internet. (Good luck if you needed help from me then with a computer problem.) But once again, with my determination and willingness to take a risk to lead our business, I now consider myself a very knowledgeable IT consultant. I now know how a network works, how to design one, and I am highly credible and regarded by my peers as a leader in a company that is on its way to great success.

I took risks time and time again to become the leader that I am today in my field, within the local, and business community even only at the age of 30. You can be 15, 18, 20, 25, 35, 40, 50, or 60 or more years old and it is never too late or too early to pursue your dreams and live out the life that you want!

Age, education, background, disabilities, or whatever excuse a lot of people use, is not a factor to pursuing success and happiness in your personal or business life. I did not let excuses stop me from pursuing what I want out of my life. It doesn't take luck, it doesn't take a rocket scientist's or a brain surgeon's knowledge for you to become a leader, be happy, fulfill your life dreams, and become successful.

It takes you and you only to be your own leader. Make decisions for yourself and not excuses!

Step out and stretch your comfort level so you can grow your leader within. Take risks and see your plans through to completion no matter what! You alone, even in your current situation, can make a change for the better. Don't let any perceived handicap or shortcoming stop you from pursuing what you want. Let your desire and passion be the reason why you pursue the things you want out of life.

Cynthia Irene Birdwise Lecocq

Cynthia has a Masters of Continuing Education -Workplace Learning and Leadership Development from the University of Calgary. She also holds a Bachelor of Science Honors (Zoology) degree from the University of Manitoba.

She has found a way to combine ecosystem sustainability through combining her knowledge of leadership development and her knowledge of biodiversity. She loves to learn continuously and arise to challenges she undertakes.

Cynthia is also an Independent Business Owner with Cyber-Wize. Her business offers her the opportunity to use her skills while creating a future foundation for research and development regarding sleep, joy and resiliency.

Cynthia has a husband, two children and four dogs in a tiny home in the middle of a tall grass prairie in the Yukon area. She says *"Life is good. Each day is a new experience. Power belongs with the people. Remember to take a chance and risk with your heart"*.

Web: www.tblast.com/4430049
Phone: 1-877-238-3739

Chapter Twenty Two

Sleep Deeply - Restful Sleep

Cynthia Irene Birdwise Lecocq

S peaking in concern for the power of energized leadership within each and every person I need to share the effect deep sleep will have on a person to help them become a fantastic leader. Why sleep? This is a book about Leadership, Success and True Happiness, right? Without a good night's sleep, your waking hours are less productive and your decision making suffers.

First of all, relax. Close your eyes and breathe deep into your belly button. Yes, I said belly button. You will likely need to practice this. Lean back a little and get yourself comfortable. Yep that's right, and smile. Now take a breath. Let it out then breathe deeper, close your eyes. Let your ribs expand and your belly fill. Well done.

At this moment you have discovered one of the necessary acts of living and that is how to breathe so oxygen will replenish your cells and all will be right with the millions of cells that are you.

Good breathing in sleep is critical to repairing and healing of all of our bodies, brains, hearts and spirits. Laughing is crucial in well-being because it makes us feel good. Feeling good about ourselves is a lost art in some places. Feeling good, breathing deeply, laughing and yes great food and love of self will help you sleep better, live well and give you the strength to be the leader you need to be in your life.

Sleeping is thought of as something that just happens. Well for shift workers and people like me sleep is a far off dream sometimes. Our systems are messed up by fooling around with our biological clocks. Sleep keeps you alive. During deep sleep your body heals itself and prepares for a new awakening after 8 hours or so. Sleep is necessary for our well-being.

When we are living with a deficit of deep sleep we react slowly. We are slow to understand the simplest things, we mess up our accounts of meetings, and of everything we attempt. It is hard.

Our power as a leader depends on our ability to be well and make good, fast decisions. Sleep is often overlooked in order to reach that late night required deadline, to feed a baby, to meet with colleagues after work and to be successful. Sleep. Can you sleep deeply?

Pressure, stress, toxic workplaces abound these days in fear of the unknown. Sleep, even deep sleep, is disturbed by dreams of terror, fear and horror. We watch television, movies and documentaries that sometimes keep us up at night. When you go to bed close all the curtains and relax into sleep. Shut off the outside world by turning off the cell phones, TVs, radios and sleep. We live in a world of noise that interferes with our body's abilities to function properly.

The power to manifest leadership comes with good, deep and restful sleep each and every night. There will be good leaders among us who sleep well, work well and give unto others in a respectful caring manner. The leaders to whom are given the gift of power know the power is a gift to be used wisely in the present moment, to be flexible like the red willow and compassionate in all ways.

True leaders seek success that has little to do with wealth in the terms of money. Leaders from within are highly successful in knowing themselves fully, being authentic, joining in learning and being respectful.

Sleep and dreams. Each night we go to bed fully expecting to awaken refreshed. Most of the people I know sleep well and are indeed refreshed. The world needs these people to dream and sleep and lead. Are you one of them?

Every person in their circle of influence has the potential to be a leader and can lead many people to becoming leaders them-selves. If we can encourage good sleep for all people we would be forging new leaders everywhere. So we need to remember to laugh, to breathe, to relax, to listen and sleep well to be who we are destined to be. True happiness comes from being centered.

Asking our Creator for guidance is one way of asking the spirit to help you. Happiness and joy go hand in hand when people feel connected to universal energy and have the necessities of life including family, shelter, clean water, wholesome food and clothing. Happiness and joy are related to who we are in this mo-ment rather than to the possessions we have.

Your dreams during sleep give you suggestions for finding your bliss and purpose in the world. So sleep well my friend, finding the leader within yourself and dreaming of success.

*"If I have seen farther than others,
it is because I was standing on the
shoulder of giants."*

Isaac Newton

Chapter Twenty Three

Conclusion

Daniel Sweet

Webster's Dictionary defines a leader as *"a person who by example, talents, or qualities of leadership plays a directing role, wields commanding influence, or has a following in any sphere or activity or thought."* It defines leadership as the ingredients of the personality that cause men and women to follow them. I sincerely hope that you feel this book has expounded on that definition quite well.

Three of the most important characteristics of leadership are dedication, charisma and enthusiasm. It is believed that every leader possesses a charisma that leads to change and success.

Leadership begins with concern, vision, and mentorship. The many co-authors in this book are showing genuine concern for your well being. They are sharing their vision with you and offering mentorship to help you find the leader within yourself.

Six Traits that Leaders Should Possess

* Good Listening Skills. This is required in order to understand employee attitudes and motivators. By asking many open-ended questions, you can really get to know those whom you are leading. When you ask questions, you have a chance to listen, and when you listen, you begin to better understand employee motivations, body language and issues. Offer challenges and solutions, and provide credit to those who provide solid, honest replies to your inquiries.

* Enthusiasm. You must, as a leader, always present a positive and energetic attitude.

* Awareness. Be aware of non-verbal's. Leaders must have a keen awareness of when followers are happy, frustrated, tired, or stressed.

* Being Decisive. Be quick and decisive with your replies. No one likes a procrastinator. Good leaders do not ponder in their decision-making; they make quick decisions to problems and find quick solutions that work.

* Rewarding. Because people desire more than monetary reward in their work, give them recognition and pats on the back for jobs done well. This sense of pride and self-worth is very important to most people.

* Positive Communication. Leaders must always create positive communication and feedback. This creates loyalty and a mutual exchange of ideas. When ideas are fresh, profits and productivity usually soar.

Making Leadership Decisions

Leaders make decisions all day long, some major and some minor. Some are bold moves, other are run-of-the-mill choices. The key is that they make them. Think of the best decisions you've made. You were most likely feeling confident and well-informed.

How does a leader gain the information needed? All good leaders surround themselves with a team of advisors. Even if you're a small business owner you have your attorney, CPA, financial advisor, etc. If you've not yet secured your team, now's the time.

You might have to search outside your inner circle to find the information you need, such as reading this book. If timing permits, seeking council from the authors found here is a great place to start.

The most effective leaders that I personally know tell me that they gather the necessary information, know when the time is right and base their decision on their 'gut.' *"It just came to me and I knew it was the right direction to proceed."* They trust in their own abilities to make informed decisions and then take action!

Creating Serious Results

Success begets more success. Declare your success. It's not bragging. It's about reeducating your thinking. Think bigger, be bolder then your previous thought. Verbally announce your success statements out loud to the universe! You are a leader, you are successful. Be bold, *"Bring it On!"* You are more powerful than the circumstances of your life. You choose your direction taking command of all your actions and decisions. The universe will respond positively.

Making sense of that feeling while you are putting that into action will increase your feeling of empowerment. Set the right goals then take the proper action.

It is about the expectation of leadership. Taking the action and having momentum, being the person of leadership that others find worthy to follow. Not only will you find leadership within yourself, others will also find leadership within you!

people need what I have.

People are willing to pay for my skills.

I have a heart for service.

I know I can succeed as a successful online tutor.

I worry about relying on Wyzant, because if they went under my clients would dry up.

As a precaution, when I build a relationship with clients that I trust, I will share information with them so that if we get separated we will know where to meet.